LIVING
WATERS

LIVING
WATERS

MESSAGES FOR LATTER-DAY DISCIPLES FROM THE LIFE AND TEACHINGS OF CHRIST

BRENT L. TOP

DESERET
BOOK

SALT LAKE CITY, UTAH

Library of Congress Cataloging-in-Publication Data

Top, Brent L.
    Living waters : messages for Latter-day disciples from the life and teachings of Christ / Brent L. Top
      p.   cm.
    Includes bibliographical references and index.
    ISBN 1-57008-830-6 (alk. paper)
    1. Christian life—Mormon authors.   I. Title.

BX8656 .T66 2002
248.4'89332—dc21

2002005479

Printed in the United States of America   7973-6962
Bang Printing, Brainerd, MN

10   9   8   7   6   5   4   3   2   1

CONTENTS

PREFACE

L iving in the Holy Land and traveling extensively throughout the Middle East has given me many new insights regarding the scriptures, as well as the cultural and political climate of the region. I have come to see that the most important natural resource in that part of the world is not the oil or natural gas or minerals or precious metals or diamonds that we typically associate with the region. Each of those commodities is an important and valuable resource in its own right; but that which is most vital and valuable—absolutely imperative—anciently and today, in the Middle East or in our own neighborhood, is water. Water gives life. It is the "life blood" of civilization. Without it, all living things would eventually wilt, wither, and die.

The changing of the seasons in the Holy Land provides a dramatic reminder of the life-giving and thirst-quenching power of water. By late summer, the many days of drying winds and scorching heat turn the hillsides brown. It appears that nothing remains alive. At times I found myself wondering what the sheep and goats that graze on those hills could actually be finding to eat. (Mark Twain must have had the same thoughts. On his visit to the Holy Land, he observed that the livestock grazed upon rocks, for there was no vegetation upon which they could dine!) Then, just when the land seems totally dead and dried, a miracle occurs. The entire landscape is dramatically transformed in a matter of weeks. From a lifeless dirty brown, the hills burst into a vibrant brilliant green, covered with spring flowers arrayed in a rainbow of colors. This remarkable metamorphosis occurs because of water—the life-giving rains of winter.

This dramatic transformation, however, is not a once-a-year witness of living waters; but, rather, a continual sign. Even in the midst of drought, and in the blazing summer heat, one can look out over the desert and barren hills and see "patches" of vegetation—like dark green spots of paint on a dusty brown canvas. In stark contrast to the surrounding desert, here and there is an oasis. Wherever there is a spring or well of water there is life.

Within this same setting two thousand years ago, the Savior used wells and water as object lessons to teach about the abundance of life and spiritual sustenance. There are two such sources of water that served as backdrops to the Master's teachings and continue to have meaning to me today. One is a well in Samaria and the other is a flowing spring on the southeastern side of the old city of Jerusalem. Two thousand years after the Savior's day, this spring and well continue to yield life-giving water. More important to me, however, these two water sources symbolize the spiritual nature of the "living waters" Jesus offers to any and all who will drink deeply from the Source.

"Whosoever drinketh of this water [meaning the water from the well] shall thirst again," Jesus declared to the Samaritan woman as she drew water from Jacob's well in the ancient city of Sychar (Shechem). "But whosoever drinketh of the water that I shall give him shall never thirst; but the water that I shall give him shall be in him a well of water springing up into everlasting life" (John 4:13–14).

The second water source I refer to is found a few hundred yards southeast of the Temple Mount in Jerusalem. It is the Gihon spring that flows into the Pool of Siloam. Although the spring had already known a long and storied past, it was especially significant and spiritually symbolic in Jesus' day. Each year as a part of the celebration of Sukkot (the Feast of Tabernacles), the Pool of

Siloam became the focus of attention of thousands of devout Jewish worshippers. On each day of the weeklong celebration, priests clothed in holy raiment would fill golden vessels with "living water" from the spring and carry them to the temple. Following behind the priests would be a solemn procession of worshippers who carried palm branches and shouted "Hosanna." The arrival at the temple was heralded with the sounding of trumpets. The water was then poured by one of the priests into a silver basin on the western side of the altar. This remarkable event was known as "the Outpouring"—symbolic of the outpouring of the Holy Spirit.[1] With this dramatic ceremony as his backdrop, "Jesus stood and cried, saying, If any man thirst, let him come unto me, and drink. He that believeth on me, as the scripture hath said, out of his belly shall flow rivers of living water" (John 7:37–38). All the trappings of the great Feast of Tabernacles, the solemn procession from the Pool of Siloam culminating in "the Outpouring"—all testified of Christ. He is the "fountain of living waters" as all the prophets and apostles have so declared (see Jeremiah 17:13; also Revelation 7:17; 1 Nephi 11:25; D&C 10:66).

Now, nearly two thousand years later, those two sources of water remain as visual reminders of what Jesus did and what he taught. There is still water drawn from Jacob's well in Samaria. I have drunk of that water and have been reminded of Jesus' words to the Samaritan woman. The water still flows from the Gihon spring to what remains today of the Pool of Siloam. I have seen the waters with my own eyes and have waded into the pool. The spring hasn't dried up and the pool is never empty. The waters are living, flowing reminders of Jesus' declaration: "I am the Living Waters."

Just as the water from those sources continues to quench the thirsty and irrigate a dried and parched land, the Savior still provides believers with "Living Waters." It is not only salvation that flows from him; his teachings continue to live and quench a thirsty world. In fact, his teachings of two millennia ago may be more relevant and necessary today. In a world that seems at times a spiritual wasteland—a desert devoid of direction and righteousness—his words continue to give life and direction to those who will drink deeply of what he has to give.

That is my purpose and hope with this book—to show how the Savior's life and teachings continue, like a constant, ever-flowing spring or well of water to give life, to heal, and to bless the spiritually thirsty—those that "hunger and thirst after righteousness." There are many lessons that can be learned from the Master and applied to our own lives. This book contains only a few—a few that have been most meaningful and relevant in my own life. I would hope that as you read some of the lessons I have learned from the "Living Waters" you will see many more lessons in your own life that have application and meaning to you. That is the greatness of "Living Waters." We can never, at least in this lifetime, learn all that he can teach us. We can never drink the fountain dry.

It is my hope that this book will inspire as well as instruct. It is my desire that the words contained herein will help to instruct in the teachings and doctrines of Christ. I am the first to recognize, however, that it is not my role or responsibility to declare doctrine. That sacred right belongs to the prophets and apostles. I sustain them wholeheartedly and try in my teachings and writings to declare "none other things than that which the prophets and apostles have written, and that which is taught them by the Comforter through the prayer of faith" (D&C 52:9). Although I have sought earnestly for that which I have written to be in harmony with and supportive of the doctrines and teachings of the Church and its leaders, I alone am responsible for the conclusions drawn and the opinions expressed. This is my own work and should not be viewed as an official publication of either The Church of Jesus Christ of Latter-day Saints or Brigham Young University. I do hope, however, that what I have written will reflect well on both institutions that I love so deeply.

Most important, however, is my desire that these chapters—these personal lessons learned from the "fountain of living waters"—will serve as a catalyst for you to personally drink from His well and to gain your own lessons from Him. What He can and will teach you is infinitely more satisfying than what I can offer. With every book that I write, I hope that my readers will gain a few new insights and applications. But most of all, I hope that when you finish reading this book you will have a greater love and appreciation for the Lord and his "inexhaustible gospel" and a renewed desire to study more intensively the scriptures and the teachings of living prophets.

I wish to express appreciation to my secretary, Cathy Higginson Owens, for her caring and diligent service in preparing the manuscript for publication. To my friends at Deseret Book I express my appreciation for their professionalism, experience, and hard work. I am especially appreciative to Cory Maxwell for his friendship and continual encouragement and Janna DeVore for her excellent editorial work. In addition, I am always grateful for the insights and help that I receive from colleagues in Religious Education at Brigham Young University. They unselfishly share ideas and provide feedback that make the end product so much better than what I could produce without them. As always, most of what ends up in the book began in the classroom. I especially express appreciation to my students for not only being the "guinea pigs" for my teachings and ideas, but also in teaching me so much—not only in word, but in the eloquence of their example. I am honored and humbled to be a teacher, for I usually am taught more than I teach.

Note

1. See Bruce R. McConkie, *The Mortal Messiah: From Bethlehem to Calvary*, 4 vols. (Salt Lake City: Deseret Book, 1979–81), 3:134–36.

CHAPTER 1

THE BARREN
FIG TREE

After I proposed marriage to my sweetheart, Wendy, and she agreed to commence her ultimate challenge and eternal "service project," we then embarked on the traditional diamond-engagement-ring-buying expedition. It was during this exciting endeavor that I not only learned a lot about diamonds (and finances) but I also learned a valuable object lesson.

Perhaps everyone who has ever purchased a diamond has had an experience similar to ours. The jeweler took us to a back room that was equipped with what looked like an oversized microscope. He then took out several small padded envelopes, each containing one diamond. "Before you make such a significant purchase, you must be taught about the Cs of diamonds," he told us as he spread the envelopes out in front of us. From the first envelope he retrieved a large, spectacular-looking diamond. I immediately saw Wendy's eyes light up, and I got worried as I mistook the sparkle in her eyes for dollar signs. "This diamond isn't worth much, and I wouldn't sell it to you," the jeweler said. "I have organized these diamonds according to their value." He pointed to the envelopes on the counter in front of us. "As you can see, this diamond is from the first envelope—meaning it is the least valuable." He could see the bewildered looks on our faces. "It may look impressive on the outside, but when you look at it closely on the inside, through this magnification lens, you will clearly see all its defects."

For the next several minutes Wendy and I received a jeweler's crash course about color, cut, clarity, and carat and how each of these characteristics determine the value of a diamond. To the naked eye there were no differences among the diamonds except for their size (carat); but when the salesman put each diamond under the microscope we could clearly distinguish the differences. The color of the diamonds ranged from pristine white to a murkish yellow. The precision of the cut of the diamond was also visible. Some diamonds were cut so precisely that the lines of the cut seemed razor sharp, whereas others looked jagged or cracked. "The precision of the cut," the jeweler explained, "is what makes the diamond sparkle." I could see the clarity of different stones as well. Some were crystal clear, and others had dark places inside the stone that ranged from large black spots to smaller defects that looked like squiggly lines. I had never realized before that the inside of a diamond was the primary determinant of its real value.

Needless to say, I didn't buy the impressive-looking diamond that we were first shown. Perhaps I could have saved a lot of money, and maybe no one else would have known that inside the showy stone were deep, dark spots, a yucky yellow color, and craggy cuts—but I would have known. Instead I bought a diamond that didn't look all that impressive—it didn't weigh Wendy's hand down with its weight. It looked pretty average, but I knew, and Wendy knew, that this diamond got high grades when it came to color, cut, and clarity—those qualities that constitute real value. Sometimes things aren't what they seem.

Many times since that experience I have thought about how much people are like diamonds. Some seem impressive on the outside, but inside they are full of all kinds of defects—some deep and dark. Others have devoted much of their time and energy to sanitizing their public personas but have given little attention to their private personas—their real selves. Some individuals may even be more like cubic zirconium; they look like diamonds but aren't actually the real thing. Then there are those people who seem average or unimpressive but are actually of the highest quality; the intents of their hearts are pure and their inward goodness blesses all around them.

The Savior often taught that true righteousness and real discipleship require the stripping away of all pretenses in our lives. He decried appearing one way and living another. The Son of Man—he who is "meek and lowly of heart"—strongly denounced, in no uncertain terms, the hypocrisy he observed in the scribes and Pharisees of his day. His teachings *then* have relevance to us *now*. The culture and context may have changed, but the concept hasn't.

Just days before his crucifixion, Jesus performed an extraordinary and unique miracle that dramatically illustrated the Master's teachings concerning outward appearances and inward goodness. While walking from the village of Bethany over the Mount of Olives to the Temple Mount in Jerusalem, a hungry Jesus noticed a fig tree in the distance and looked forward to enjoying the refreshment and sweetness that a ripe fig would provide.

"And seeing a fig tree afar off having leaves, he came, if haply he might find any thing thereon: and when he came to it, *he found nothing but leaves*; for the time of figs was not yet.

"And Jesus answered and said unto it, No man eat fruit of thee hereafter for ever. And his disciples heard it" (Mark 11:13–14; emphasis added).

The very next day as Jesus and the disciples once again walked the familiar path to Jerusalem, "they saw the fig tree dried up from the roots" (Mark 11:20). The disciples remembered what Jesus had spoken concerning the tree that was all leaves and no fruit and were amazed at how quickly and completely the tree had died.

This miracle is unique in that, as far as we can ascertain from the scriptures, it is the only miracle of condemnation performed by the Savior—an act that was intended to destroy, not to help or heal. Although it was destructive in nature, Jesus' cursing of the barren fig tree was intended to teach an important lesson to his disciples: pretty leaves mean nothing when fruit is what is desired or required. The cursing of this unproductive fig tree was not the first time Jesus had taught this principle, but it was perhaps the most unforgettable. It was but an exclamation point to the Lord's earlier condemnations of any form of hypocrisy—shows devoid of substance, appearances devoid of righteousness, flashiness devoid of faithfulness.

The barren fig tree represents those individuals or institutions who appear to be righteous, faithful, and committed to doing good, but in reality are not. The scriptures call this attribute *hypocrisy* and those who possess it *hypocrites*. In our modern-day vernacular are phrases we often use to characterize hypocrites:

- "They don't practice what they preach."
- "They talk the talk, but don't walk the walk."
- "They are all show and no go!"
- "They say one thing and do another."

The word in ancient Greek from which our English word *hypocrisy* derives is *hypokrisis*. It is a word that has the Greek theater at its heart. It literally refers to the art of acting, or playing a role in a dramatic performance. The Greek word *hypocrites* means actors. In fact, actors who were called upon to play the role of a woman, an animal, or a mythological god had to use a mask to cover their faces. The masking of an actor was known as hypocrisy, for it allowed him to pretend to be something he clearly was not.

"Woe unto you . . . hypocrites!" (Matthew 23:27) were the thundering words of the Son of God. With these words, the Master did not condemn the innocent who were acting a fictitious role in a dramatic presentation with the sole purpose of entertaining an audience. He condemned those who were intentionally living a double life. Their hypocrisy was not for entertainment but deception; it was not an innocent mask worn in a play but a personal life that lacked authenticity and integrity. Hypocrisy, like diamonds in a jeweler's showcase, comes in many shapes, sizes, and shades. There is zirconium-like hypocrisy, where one appears to be the "real thing" of righteousness but in reality doesn't possess the requisite spiritual substance. At the other end of the hypocrisy continuum are those who may not blatantly be living a double life but who do the right things for the wrong reasons. They are like real diamonds that sparkle on the outside but possess flaws on the inside. The flaws are the less-than-righteous motives and intents for the outward actions of keeping the commandments. This is the hypocrisy of professing to really know God but not having come to that personal relationship (see D&C 112:26).

Like pride, hypocrisy, in all its many masks, is easily seen in others but difficult to see within ourselves. It is even more difficult to root out of our lives and hearts when it is found. As disciples of Christ we have covenanted to "follow the Son, with full purpose of heart, *acting no hypocrisy and no deception before God*" (2 Nephi 31:13; emphasis added). As we seek to faithfully follow and genuinely emulate him, we should take inventory of our lives and strip away the masks we sometimes wear that prevent us from truly being what we profess to be and bearing the fruit he desires of us.

LIVING A DOUBLE LIFE: PRETENDING TO BE MORE RIGHTEOUS THAN WE REALLY ARE

Jesus cursed the barren fig tree because all of its energies went to producing large, beautiful leaves instead of sweet fruit. It took nutrients from the soil, light from the sun, and valuable water from a parched desert clime. In turn, it produced foliage but no figs. It was never intended to be merely a shade tree. I can't imagine Jesus cursing a little, fledgling tree that tried with all its might to produce figs but could not because it lacked something vital to the process. It was cursed and withered and died because it had never intended to bear fruit, but only to look good. It was not what it "professed" to be. It might as well have had a sign posted on its trunk: "What you see is *not* what you get."

This common form of hypocrisy—pretending to be something better than we are—was the central focus of one of the Savior's most stinging rebukes of the scribes and Pharisees.

"Woe unto you, scribes and Pharisees, hypocrites! for ye are like unto whited sepulchres, which indeed appear beautiful outward, but are within full of dead men's bones, and of all uncleanness.

"Even so ye also outwardly appear righteous unto men, but within ye are full of hypocrisy and iniquity" (Matthew 23:27–28).

There can be no mistaking how Jesus felt about this form of hypocrisy. The simile he used—comparing them to "whited sepulchres"—is most interesting. Under Mosaic law, a devout Jew became ritually unclean through contact with the dead. Death and decay symbolized a spiritual uncleanness and estrangement from God. The Lord compared the hypocrite to someone who knows that the tomb contains the very elements of uncleanness yet masks it by painting the outside and landscaping the area to disguise the real nature of the structure. This is similar to a person making his life look like a pleasant little garden of pretty flowers when it is really a stinking cesspool of sin.

Being a disciple of Christ requires real righteousness—not just an attempt to "play the part." There should be little, if any, gap between what we "preach" and how we "practice" the principles of the gospel. Because none of us is perfect, there will always be areas for needed improvement—areas in which our behavior doesn't correspond with our ideals as closely as we would like. But our desires and efforts to improve—however feeble they may be—will point us in the right direction. We cannot live like the fictional Jekyll and Hyde—acting good by day and evil by night. Such a double life is a spiritual form of the business deception known as "bait and switch," where you advertise one thing but deliver something much different and far inferior to that which was shown.

In modern revelation, the Lord speaks of those who "undertake to cover [their] sins" (D&C 121:37). I find that an interesting phrase. How can you "cover" sins? Certainly, hiding them behind a mask covers them. Such actions are the natural man's attempts to make sins go away by publicly pretending to be different from how he really is. The truth of the matter is, however, that when the mask comes down the sins remain. Righteousness requires authenticity in gospel living, not artistic ability in mask making. The Prophet Joseph Smith summarized this concept in a unique and thought-provoking way: "I love that man better who swears a stream as long as my arm yet deals justice to his neighbors and mercifully deals his substance to the poor, than the long, smooth-faced hypocrite."[1]

There can be no double standards in discipleship, no preaching and expecting others to live by one standard of righteousness while thinking ourselves above the law and living a life contrary to the standard we supposedly espouse. I once had this lesson impressed upon me in a somewhat unique and humbling way—"out of the mouth of babes." Several years ago when our children were little, we had a family "video party." Each of the children had been allowed to pick out their favorite video to watch and we also had selected one or two that we wanted to view. After we had spent the day watching videos and eating popcorn and treats, I told the kids that it was late and time for them to go to bed.

"Why do we have to go to bed now?" my son, Justin, asked. "There is still another video to watch." I had rented a video for Wendy and me to watch together. It was not a bad film, nor was it risqué; but it did have a more mature theme. I didn't think it would be wise to let the children watch it.

"You guys can't watch this one. It's for Mom and Dad and it's not good for kids," I reasoned.

Justin's response was most profound for a young boy. "Well, if it is not good for us to watch, why can you watch it?"

Now don't get me wrong—I recognize that sometimes there is a need for entertainment and activities on a higher intellectual level than *Sesame Street, Power Rangers,* or Barney, the loveable purple dinosaur. I have watched *Sleeping Beauty* so many times that I can recite the dialogue backwards. I also understand that some things my kids just love cause my brain to turn into jelly; likewise, my kids may feel the same way about my favorite movies, music, or television programs. That is not the real issue here. Justin's words made me really stop and think about the message I was giving him. I could have tried to explain away the whole matter and all its different implications, but no matter what I said, it would still appear that there was a double standard—that goodness, morality, right and wrong meant something different for Mom and Dad. I have come to realize that no movie is good enough to be worth leaving the wrong idea in the impressionable minds of my children. Maybe Justin had it right—maybe his idea really speaks to what is most important. If it's not good for my kids, what makes it good for me? Am I willing to eliminate any form of hypocrisy from my life so that my children will know that there are no double standards in the gospel—what God expects of them, he expects also of me?

If I teach my children to be honest and expect them so to be, then I must be honest and true. If I advocate moral purity and virtuous thoughts, then I must be clean. If I want my children to pray and repent, so must I. If as a bishop I counsel husbands and wives to show more love and respect to each other, I should do the same. What is *said* at the pulpit must also be *lived* in private. Unfortunately, we are all familiar with someone—fathers or mothers, husbands or wives, sons or daughters, brothers or sisters, neighbors or friends—of whom it could be said, "He/she is a different person behind closed doors." We all behave differently in private to some degree, and thankfully so. We would not want all of our dirty laundry—our irritating idiosyncrasies, annoying habits, and dumb jokes—to be seen and heard by all. When it comes to gospel living, however, what you see *should be* what you get. Our private lives, our dealings with others, and our relationship with God should correlate with our public image.

Several years ago an ad for a well-known product appeared on television featuring a popular sports figure. The slogan that was supposed to hook viewers was: "Image is everything!" *What a dumb slogan*, I thought. How stupid do they think we are? I would rather have a quality product that does what I want it to do than an inferior product that makes me feel cool by buying it. When it comes to pleasing God, image is nothing—genuine gospel living is everything. When we are the "real deal" of righteousness, the image will take care of itself.

GOOD BUT NOT TOO GOOD: PRETENDING TO BE LESS DEVOUT THAN WE REALLY ARE

There is another kind of hypocrisy of which we rarely speak or think, but it is, nonetheless, a form of putting on a mask and acting in a manner different from who or what we really are. "While casual members are not unrighteous," Elder Neal A. Maxwell observed, "they often avoid appearing to be too righteous by seeming less committed than they really are—an ironic form of hypocrisy."[2] Unfortunately, we see many people in the Church who seek to straddle the line between putting their light under a bushel and holding it up high for all to see. They do not want to be bad, do evil, or influence others to be wicked, but neither do they want to be "too good" or viewed as a goody-goody. This common character trait—appearing to be less than we really are—less committed to the gospel, less righteous—is a form of hypocrisy that also prevents us from standing tall as real disciples of Christ. President

N. Eldon Tanner of the First Presidency, spoke of this other kind of hypocrisy.

"Too often . . . we see members of the Church who in their hearts know and believe, but through fear of public opinion fail to stand up and be counted. This kind of hypocrisy is as serious as the other; it makes it difficult for others to respect us, and often adversely affects or influences the lives of other members of the Church who expect us to stand by our commitments to the Church and not hesitate to manifest our faith."[3]

Just as the barren fig tree—symbolic of hypocrisy—sent out false signals, we do the same when we appear less religious and righteous than we are on the inside. That is another form of the "bait and switch." I may leave the impression that I have no problem with immorality or dishonesty or any other vice, when in reality I would never engage in such behaviors. It is passive hypocrisy to dress and act like the worldly and the wicked, and then become offended if our signals attract the wrong kind of attention. It is passive hypocrisy to put on the mask of dancing and dining in the great spacious building, but still desire to cling to the iron rod. Whenever we are unwilling to let our lives accurately reflect our love for the Savior and our allegiance to his gospel, we are hypocrites—actors putting on a mask to be seen as something we are not.

TO BE SEEN OF MEN:
DOING THE RIGHT THINGS FOR THE WRONG REASONS

There is another kind of hypocrisy that Jesus directly and forcefully condemned in the Sermon on the Mount. This form of hypocrisy is subtle yet insidious, because it is almost unrecognizable. And, if not eradicated, it can fatally flaw the human heart. On its face, Jesus' rebuke of these type of hypocrites seems somewhat ironic, for he was condemning the most religious, the most observant, and those whom many considered to be the very role models of devout Judaism. They were doing all the right things, such as fasting, praying, serving in leadership positions, and contributing alms for the poor. It was not so much *what* these hypocrites were doing that Jesus denounced as it was *why* they were doing what they were doing. It was the inner motivation for their righteous acts that he questioned. It was not their actions, or lack of them, which constituted their hypocrisy; rather, it was their unrighteous motives. Motivations and intentions speak loudly about who it is we really love and desire to serve and from whom we desire approbation. Jesus' words, given two millennia ago overlooking the Sea of Galilee, are as relevant now to Latter-day Saints as they were when directed to disciples in former days:

"Take heed that ye do not your alms before men, *to be seen of them*: otherwise ye have no reward of your Father which is in heaven.

"Therefore when thou doest thine alms, do not sound a trumpet before thee, as the hypocrites do in the synagogues and in the streets, that they may have glory of men. Verily I say unto you, They have their reward.

"But when thou doest alms, let not thy left hand know what thy right hand doeth:

"That thine alms may be in secret: and thy Father which seeth in secret himself shall reward thee openly.

"And when thou prayest, thou shalt not be as the hypocrites are: for they love to pray standing in the synagogues and in the corners of the streets, *that they may be seen of men*. Verily I say unto you, They have their reward.

"But thou, when thou prayest, enter into thy closet, and when thou hast shut thy door, pray to thy Father which is in secret; and thy Father which seeth in secret shall reward thee openly.

"But when ye pray, use not vain repetitions, as the [hypocrites] do: for they think *that they shall be heard* for their much speaking.

"Be not ye therefore like unto them: for your Father knoweth what things ye have need of, before ye ask him. . . .

"Moreover when ye fast, be not, as the hypocrites, of a sad countenance: for they disfigure their faces, *that they may appear* unto men to fast. Verily I say unto you, They have their reward.

"But thou, when thou fastest, anoint thine head, and wash thy face;

"That thou appear not unto men to fast, but unto thy Father which is in secret: and thy Father, which seeth in secret, shall reward thee openly" (Matthew 6:1–8, 16–18; emphasis added).

Jesus' opening caution to "take heed" seems to imply that it is a universal tendency of the natural man to do things in order to receive recognition, honors, and acceptance of others. When we do *higher* things for *lower* reasons we are guilty of a form of hypocrisy, of playing a part that isn't really us. In a way, this hypocrite is also a "whited sepulchre"—appearing good on the outside but not so great on the inside. The difference, however, is that one kind of hypocrite acts one way in a particular setting and behaves in an opposite manner in another setting. The hypocrite Jesus speaks of in the preceding verses doesn't necessarily lead a double-life or hide evil actions; but inside the "whited sepulchre" of his life are improper motivations and intentions masked behind outward actions of goodness. The Savior urges his followers, both ancient and modern, to overcome this natural-man tendency and become more like him by doing the right things for the right reasons. "We must not only *do* what is right. We must act for the right reasons," Elder Dallin H. Oaks wrote. "It is easier to have clean hands than to have a pure heart. It is easier to control our acts than to control our thoughts. The requirement that our good acts must be accompanied by good motives is subtle and difficult in practice."[4]

Just as the scribes and Pharisees did good and noble acts not out of their love for God but primarily to be seen of men and to receive the recognition of the world, there is almost a universal temptation for us in the Church today to unwittingly do the same. While I cannot judge the motivations and intents of others, I know my own weaknesses. The hypocrisy that can easily creep into my life if I am careless is not the type that requires me to live a double life; most of us, in fact, are usually on guard for obvious hypocrisy. I must take care to avoid the subtle hypocrisy that comes from doing right things not because they are right, but because I want to impress others or receive some extrinsic reward or validation for my service. While I may have, somewhere in the back of my mind, a desire to please God and be righteous, there is often a more immediate underlying motivation that drives me. It is this form of hypocrisy which I must constantly guard against and eradicate whenever it shows its ugly form in my life. I am quite confident that I am not the only one who has to struggle with this weakness. Thus, in our quest to become more Christlike, deep personal introspection is needed. As we seek to "cleanse the inner vessel" and examine not only our actions and thoughts, but also the motives for our actions, it would be beneficial to consider the following question: "Why am I doing this?" Elder Oaks believes this question should be a guidepost for us along the path of discipleship.

"We can work to reform our motives if we are continually asking ourselves: Why am I taking this action? That question is especially important for actions that we suppose to be good. It reminds us that it is not enough to act in ways that seem to be good. We must act for the right reasons. If we truly desire to please God and serve him, continual self-examination of our reasons for actions cannot fail to expose our selfish and sordid motives and challenge us to reform them."[5]

This "continual self-examination" advocated by Elder Oaks may be as painful as it is instructive. Yet, it can be a valuable prescription for spiritual well-being in our constant efforts to follow the Master in "acting no hypocrisy." We can and should apply this reality check to a myriad of practical everyday situations in which we find ourselves. I have struggled with the question "Why am I doing this?" in numerous circumstances and settings. Such difficult, yet much needed, self-examination may include many, if not all, of the following real-life questions:

- Do I seek to outdo others in my Church calling?
- Do I feel some sense of competition or comparison with others?
- Do I feel a pang of envy when others receive certain callings or receive recognitions or awards?
- When I share personal spiritual experiences, am I doing so under the influence and prompting of the Spirit for the edification of others, or am I trying to impress people with how "spiritual" I am?
- Is my service in the Church dependent upon being in high profile positions, or would I still faithfully magnify my calling if I were serving where no one would see or notice my efforts?
- Do I perform anonymous and unheralded service that goes beyond mere involvement in organized ward or quorum service projects?
- Are my comments in church meetings motivated out of sincere hungering and thirsting after gospel knowledge and a humble desire to contribute to others' understanding, or are they more to show off how much I know or to set straight the comments of someone else?
- Do I bear my testimony in testimony meeting out of a genuine spiritual desire to praise God and testify of those sacred truths that have been revealed, or am I using it as a forum to impress others?
- Do I find myself most concerned about maintaining an image—either in the Church or in my profession? Do I think

more about how a certain action will affect that image rather than what is right?

- Am I motivated more by the praises of men and the status of position than by the quiet assurance that the Lord is mindful and accepting of my efforts?

Some of these questions are extremely difficult to answer, and often there is a fine line between altruistic and self-serving behaviors. I believe that is the very point Jesus is trying to make in condemning the hypocrites and calling his disciples to a higher form of righteousness. The hypocrisy of doing the right things because of impure motives infects our souls, however slowly and subtly. As we ponder the miracle of the cursing of the barren fig tree and consider the Savior's teachings, we are impelled to assess our motives and priorities. As painful as it may be, we must seek to be perfectly honest with ourselves regarding our true motivations. We cannot be truly righteous and bear the fruit of genuine faithfulness with supposedly good actions that are performed for the wrong reasons, out of an impure heart. "Acting no hypocrisy" requires not only a purification of *what* I do, but also *why* I do it.

> *Cleanse first that which is within the cup and platter,*
> *that the outside of them may be clean also.*
> —Matthew 23:26

The Savior invites us to become more like him inwardly as well as outwardly. To be his devoted disciples and fruitful contributors in his kingdom, we cannot be like the barren fig tree—all leaves and no fruit. He wants us to be like diamonds that sparkle to the naked eye and are pure within as well. He beckons us to search our souls and do some serious housecleaning, sweeping hypocrisy, in any of its forms, from every nook and cranny of our lives. He desires of us both clean hands—in public and private—and pure hearts. He desires us to take off the masks, quit the role-playing, and be genuine Saints. That is the spiritual lesson Jesus taught his disciples when, with a unique and powerful miracle, he cursed the barren fig tree.

Notes

1. Joseph Smith, *The Teachings of Joseph Smith*, ed. Larry E. Dahl and Donald Q. Cannon (Salt Lake City: Bookcraft, 1997), 333.
2. Neal A. Maxwell, in Conference Report, October 1992, 89.
3. N. Eldon Tanner, in Conference Report, October 1970, 53.
4. Dallin H. Oaks, *Pure in Heart* (Salt Lake City: Bookcraft, 1988), 15, 18.
5. Ibid., 148.

CHAPTER 2

CHOOSING THE
GOOD PART

Afew years ago I was asked to deliver a number of lectures and presentations to several stakes in the Pacific Northwest. I was pleased that my wife, Wendy, could also accompany me. To our surprise, our hosts had booked us in one of the nicest hotels in the area. During the years I had worked for the Church Educational System and BYU, we had generally stayed in more modest motels—what might be characterized as "budget accommodations." I had never stayed in such a nice hotel before— but I didn't complain! The morning after my speaking assignments, before we departed for the airport, we went to the hotel restaurant for breakfast. Instead of the usual bowl of cereal, muffin, or fat-free bagel offered by most hotels, we were dumbfounded to discover an exquisite brunch-buffet, unlike any we had ever seen before. There were more tables with different kinds of foods than most buffets have items. There were the traditional breakfast items—waffles, omelets, fruits, sausage, ham, hash browns, and eggs Benedict. There was cold cereal—I didn't waste my time on that! And there were other tables loaded with equally sumptuous delights. The salad table must have had twenty different kinds of salad—green salads, Caesar salad, pasta salads, potato salad, fruit salads—every kind of salad imaginable, with the exception of a traditional Mormon green-Jell-O-and-grated-carrot salad! The seafood table caught my attention immediately—lobster Newburg, steamed crab legs, shrimp, grilled halibut, smoked salmon, clams, mussels (and I needed muscles!). In addition, there were several main course entrees—chicken dishes, roast turkey and ham, prime rib of beef—as well as potatoes, rice, and every kind of cooked vegetable imaginable. To top things off, I was offered all the fresh-squeezed orange juice and soda pop I desired. While I was mentally plotting how I could put shrimp and crab on the "endangered species" list, Wendy discovered the dessert buffet. O my goodness! I had never seen anything like that before.

Everything looked absolutely heavenly, but there was one *big* problem. I didn't know where to begin. I knew I had to have a plan—and most of that plan was not to waste any time or space on waffles, salads, or breads. I didn't need the "filler"—I was saving my stomach for the "good stuff." I immediately recognized that I would have to pace myself. I would have to have the best stuff (things that I couldn't afford to order if I was paying)—and by all means I had to save room for dessert! The plan sounded so good to my head, but when I stood before those buffet tables, my stomach didn't agree. There were so many wonderful things to choose from. Where should I start? How could I pass up anything? Everything looked fabulous! How could I ever save room for dessert? I wondered if I should perhaps start with dessert. I was confused! Even though I was in "Gastronomical Shangri-la," I could not fully enjoy this eating experience, because there were too many good things. Because I could not eat them all to my complete satisfaction—my eyes being bigger than my stomach, my desires bigger than my capacity—it actually detracted from the whole experience. It was a startling realization that too many good things can in some ways become a bad thing.

Let me now share with you another experience. It too uses food as one of its central themes (you can tell what is on my mind most of the time). This is not a specific experience, but a general or composite one that characterizes what we have experienced in our family many times before. I must tell you up front that I really enjoy cooking. I find it relaxing. When I cook I can clear my head of the stresses, concerns, and worries of the day and focus completely on what I am preparing. (I once heard Wendy tell a group of young women about my love for cooking. She then encouraged them to marry a man that cooks, for, as she said, "it covers a multitude of sins." Now that I think about it, I'm not sure she was complimenting my cooking or commenting on my "multitude of sins.") Perhaps you love to cook as well, so you will understand what I mean when I say that I always start out loving to cook, but don't always finish up with that same passion. Let me illustrate.

At our house, a family celebration cannot be had unless there is also a huge family dinner. We may be celebrating the return of a son or daughter from a mission, the marriage of a child, or it might just be a family reunion of sorts. It may be that family members have traveled a great distance to be together, or, as is often the case with our family, it may be the first time in many years that all of the extended family have been together. Whatever the circumstances, it is a joyous and momentous occasion. Yet, it doesn't come easy. Even something this significant has its cost—a cost we don't always plan for or count on.

Before the guests arrive there is the planning of the menu, buying the food—which entails shopping not in just one store, but going from one to another to get the best deals. The house must be cleaned from top to bottom. You certainly wouldn't want your mother-in-law to find any dust on the shelves or fingerprints on the windows. When it comes time to prepare the dinner, there is cutting and chopping to be done, the dinner table must be set just right, gravy has to be made (without lumps), and, of course, there must be a centerpiece—not just any centerpiece—it must be seasonally appropriate and color-coordinated. Does this ring a bell?

At my house, there is more work in the kitchen than one person can do. And I often feel that the burden to do the work is placed on my shoulders alone. My head starts to throb from all the hurrying and scurrying and all the laughing and playing and noise that fills the house. *How can the kids be having such a good time? Don't they notice me killing myself for them in the kitchen?* I always wonder. Can you see yourself in this picture?

When the dinner is ready and placed on the table, everyone comments on how beautiful it looks and how good it smells. After the blessing the chaos begins again—people dive into the food like there is no tomorrow. By this time I begin to wonder what we are celebrating anyway. *Why did I invite these people here?* Everyone else is devouring the meal and commenting on how delicious everything is, but I have almost always lost my appetite. I don't want to eat. I just want peace and quiet. I want the relatives to go home. I want to crash on the bed. Why has the family feast of celebration, planned with such high hopes and intended to be a time of rejoicing, actually become such a burden, filled with frustration and fatigue? Perhaps the answer is found in the fact that all the preparations I made that I thought were so important—that I felt were so vital to the success of the event—weren't really necessary after all. The lesson in this is that doing far more than what is essential causes us to lose our focus on what matters most. And when we lose focus, we are easily distracted, which results in frustration rather than fulfillment.

There is an episode recorded in the New Testament which illustrates both of these dilemmas and teaches us concerning what matters most. You are familiar with the details of the story of Mary and Martha, but do you really understand the principles the Savior was teaching them and us? It is much more than a story. It is much more than a gentle chiding of conscientious Martha. Contained in this ancient account is a message for a modern world. It may be a simple story, but it is relevant for us today—vital for our emotional and spiritual survival in these challenging times. In Luke 10:38 the story begins:

"Now it came to pass, as they went, that [Christ] entered into a certain village: and a certain woman named Martha received him into her house.

"And she had a sister called Mary, which also sat at Jesus' feet, and heard his word.

"But Martha was cumbered about much serving, and came to him, and said, Lord, dost thou not care that my sister hath left me to serve alone? bid her therefore that she help me."

Let me interject an item for your consideration at this point. Culturally speaking, Martha has good reason to be upset with her sister. Anciently (and even in some Palestinian settings today) the women did not intermingle socially with the men. The women would gather together preparing the meal—eating by themselves and mingling among the other women in the party, but not associating with the men—even if the guest of honor was speaking in the other room. So Martha is asking Jesus to remind Mary of "her place." But how does Jesus respond?

"And Jesus answered and said unto her, Martha, Martha [you know you're in big trouble if someone says your name twice!], thou art careful and troubled about many things:

"But one thing is needful: and Mary hath chosen that good part, which shall not be taken away from her" (Luke 10:38–42).

This story is often misquoted and misinterpreted. First, the misquote: I have heard people say a zillion times—"Mary chose the *better* part." It doesn't say that—it says "that *good* part"—in fact, some Bible translations say "the *best* part." I have often heard people use this scriptural story to justify not doing housework, saying that it is *better* to devote yourself to associating with good people and pursuing intellectual or spiritual learning than worrying about a clean house. They want to pit Mary *the learner* against Martha *the housekeeper*. That is not the intent of the story at all! What is it that Jesus wants us to learn from this experience? What application can we draw from Jesus' words that will have meaning to us amidst the stresses and struggles of modern society? Important concepts emerge as we examine more closely some of the words and phrases in Jesus' tender teaching of his friend, Martha.

"*Martha was cumbered.*" One translation of the word *cumbered* is "perplexed" or "frustrated."[1] What was the source of her frustration? At first glance it looks as though she was perplexed and annoyed by Mary's unwillingness to help, but there seems to be something else that is bothering her. Martha was frustrated—or, as one translation says, "harassed"—by all the different cares and demands placed on her, pulling her in different directions at the same time. It was not a choice between good and bad or sin and righteousness, but rather the difficulty of having to decide between too many good things, too many *good* choices.[2] Elder Neal A. Maxwell taught: "So often our hardest choices are between competing and desirable alternatives (each with righteous consequences), when there is *not* time to do both at once. Indeed, it is at the mortal intersections—where time and talent and opportunities meet—that priorities, like traffic lights, are sorely needed. Quiet, sustained goodness is the order of heaven, not conspicuous but episodic busyness."[3]

THE DEVIL'S DANGEROUS DOCTRINE OF DISTRACTION

Just as I was perplexed with how to proceed at that magnificent brunch buffet, we often find ourselves frustrated because there are so many good things we want to do—or perhaps feel we should do—that we cannot do them all. The Savior told Martha, "Thou art careful and troubled about many things." He was acknowledging her conscientiousness but also reminding her that her conscientiousness in some ways had become a weakness. The phrase "troubled about many things" could also be interpreted as, "You are distracted. Your attention and efforts are divided, and, as a result, all that you do is less effective." In our day, the Lord has commanded us to be "anxiously engaged in a good cause" (D&C 58:27), but that doesn't mean we have to be anxiously engaged in *every* good cause. Trying to do all things or be all things to all people all the time results in Martha-like frustration. I believe we must learn, like Martha, that being cumbered with over-involvement in too many good causes can actually divert us away from the things that matter most. Martha wasn't sinning or being evil in any way. All of her efforts and attentions were drawn to doing good for someone else (in this particular case, the Savior). But instead of finding fulfillment and peace and joy in her labors, she was more frustrated and worn out than ever. *She thinks the problem is Mary*—for not helping out with all of the preparations—*but the real problem is Martha herself*—for being over-involved and distracted from that which mattered most.

Martha was "cumbered about much serving." Serving is a good thing. Yet, when that useful activity takes us—our hearts and minds and souls—away from that which the original service or activity was intended to bring us to, we are left harassed—frustrated. *Good things can take away better things.* As Elder Maxwell said, "Some choices are *diversions* more than they are transgressions. As a result of these diversions, the sins of omission mount up. And they constitute a real *deprivation* because of what we withhold from our fellow human beings. Perhaps it is unintentional, but without that first commandment [to love God with all our heart, might, mind, and strength], some things get omitted."[4]

How many things in your life—good, desirable, honorable, righteous things—are actually getting in the way of the "good part," an intimate relationship with God? As C. S. Lewis wrote, "God wants to give us something, but cannot, because our hands are full—there's nowhere for Him to put it."[5] Many times these other things that fill our hands and our lives are not worldly or wicked things, but needful things, things that cannot be ignored—as one religious leader called them, they are "the tyranny of the urgents." We can all relate to Martha to some degree—pushed and pulled in many directions and by many different demands—most of which are not only good but also necessary. The end result can still be the same—distraction, frustration, and spiritual and emotional burnout. Speaking to the women of the Church, Elder M. Russell Ballard of the Quorum of the Twelve made some interesting observations that can benefit both women and men in today's world:

"Some of you very likely are striving to be 'supermoms.' You feel the need to spend time with your husband and children. You want to be sure to have family prayer, read the scriptures, and have family home evening. You also feel the need to help children with homework and music lessons; keep your home presentable; prepare nutritious meals; keep clothes clean and mended; chauffeur children and possibly their friends to school and to a variety of lessons, practices, and games; and keep everyone in the family on schedule, making sure they are where they should be when they should be there. And that is all within your family and home. It makes me weary just reviewing all this! It doesn't include PTA, volunteer service, or caring for family members who are ill or aged. You feel the need to protect your family from the many evil influences in the world such as suggestive television, films, and videos; alcohol; drugs; and pornography. You are committed to and faithfully fulfill your Church callings. In addition, many of you must earn a living because financial pressures are real and cannot be ignored. If anything is left or neglected, you may feel that you have failed. . . .

". . . I saw a bumper sticker the other day . . . that may say it all:

"'God put me on earth to accomplish a certain number of things. Right now I am so far behind, I will never die!'"[6]

When I was growing up in Idaho Falls, Idaho, my father owned a fabric store. That wasn't bad in and of itself, but what made life somewhat difficult for me was that my Dad believed strongly in hard work, and he insisted that I work, and work hard. Unfortunately for me that meant my place of work for several years was his fabric store. As a teenage boy I would rather have had leprosy than work in a fabric store! (It could have been worse, however, because a few years later my Dad bought another business—a maternity wear store.) I know more about fabrics, buttons, zippers, and patterns—Butterick, McCall's, Vogue, and Simplicity—than most women in the world today! While I must admit I haven't had to use that knowledge much in life, there was one lesson I learned in that fabric store that has stayed with me all my life. Four times a year we had to take inventory of the patterns—pulling out the out-of-fashion patterns and replacing them with new ones. Once a year we had to take inventory of everything in the store. Can you imagine how many buttons, eye-fasteners, snaps, and zippers there are in a fabric store—in addition to the yards and yards of taffeta, velvet, broadcloth, and corduroy? I learned how important—more than important—how vital it is to take periodic inventory of our lives, discarding those things of lesser value and replacing them with the essential things.

Just as Martha was, we need to be stopped dead in our tracks once in a while and examine *what* we are doing and *why* we are doing it. Eternal priorities absolutely must guide our lives and actions and choices—for without them we will end up being cumbered, perplexed, and frustrated that we are spending our time and resources on lesser matters at the exclusion of celestial values. Satan realizes that he cannot always use his heavy arsenal of temptations to be immoral or dishonest or violent on good, conscientious people. These "fiery darts" would probably have little, if any, immediate effect on faithful people who are diligently striving to be righteous. He knows that he will be far more successful with us if he can get us frustrated by our inability to do all the good things we would like (or sometimes feel that we have to do). I believe this is the very thing Jesus was warning Martha about—the devil's dangerous doctrine of distraction. It doesn't seem as dangerous as many of his other temptations, but the end product is often the same. We become lost in the mists of darkness of the world, because we have been distracted and have looked "beyond the mark." Elder William R. Bradford of the Seventy counseled the Saints in general conference to unclutter their lives of such diversionary encumbrances. "We need to examine all the ways we use our time," he taught, "our work, our ambitions, our affiliations, and the habits that drive our actions. As we make such a study, we will be able to better understand what we should really be spending our time doing. . . .

"A mother should never allow herself to become so involved with extras that she finds herself neglecting her divine role. A father must not let any activity, no matter how interesting or important it may seem, keep him from giving of himself in the one-on-one service and close, constant care of each member of the family."[7]

A few years ago, I attended a meeting in the Tabernacle in Salt Lake City with religious educators from the Church Educational System. Elder Jeffrey R. Holland of the Council of the Twelve spoke to us. After his address, which was broadcast all around the world via satellite, there was a question-answer session for the people gathered in the Tabernacle. Elder Holland said that one of the most commonly asked questions he faces around the Church is "How can we do it all?" He then told of an experience he had in hearing the counsel of President Gordon B. Hinckley at a stake conference in the Salt Lake Valley. After watching the mothers in the congregation (who Elder Holland called the "Cheerios Brigade") wrestle children, quiet crying babies, and try to listen to the talks—all while the husbands were totally oblivious to the chaos about them—President Hinckley rose to address the large audience. "It is really, really tough being a mother," he said. "I don't know how you can do it all!" This prophet of God then counseled these good women (as well as the men) to keep their priorities straight, so they could do what the Lord would want them to do. He listed four priorities in order of importance. His words to us today are as vital as the words that Jesus declared to Martha when she was *cumbered*—torn and tugged in many directions, perplexed, and frustrated by all of the demands placed upon her. While not each of these priorities will apply equally to everyone, the principles are universal. President Hinckley's four priorities were these:

1. *Spiritual and emotional strength for each individual.* Studying the scriptures and personal prayer are vital to spiritual health and well-being. "You will never have anything to offer to others," President Hinckley said, "if you don't feed yourself spiritually and keep yourself emotionally strong." When our children were young, Wendy used to collapse on the floor after putting the kids to bed and say, "I've been 'Mommied' to death!" She often felt, and still does at times, like a sponge that has been squeezed dry of every possible molecule of water. When the sponge is wrung out it must be immersed and filled up again. Even the Savior periodically withdrew himself from the crowds to seek his Father and to become refreshed and rejuvenated spiritually, emotionally, and physically so he could minister to those who so desperately needed him (see Luke 5:16). So must you and I personally and individually. Scripture study, daily prayer, quiet time to think and meditate—focusing on what really matters most to the Lord—is vital to your spiritual and emotional health. You can't afford to neglect these things, because not only will you suffer, but others will suffer, because you will have so much less to offer them. Running faster and doing more may actually be counterproductive at times. Like a mouse on the treadmill, we often run around faster and faster, but never get where we want to be. Sometimes this is because we aren't taking care of our spirits and our minds as we should.

In the New Testament, the apostle Paul warned that in the last days there would be some who were "ever learning, and never able to come to the knowledge of the truth" (2 Timothy 3:7). Perhaps we may be guilty of something similar if we are "ever meeting"— ever coming and going—ever holding activities, but never coming to the knowledge of God. Perhaps we should pause to pray not that we can run faster in order to do more, but that we might respond to the Savior's invitation to spiritually "lie down in green pastures" and walk "beside still waters." If we can't slow down long enough for the Lord to catch up to us, how can he "restoreth our souls" (Psalm 23)? One of my favorite poems reflects this concept. It is entitled "Slow Me Down, Lord."

> *Slow me down, Lord!*
> *Ease the pounding of my heart*
> *By the quieting of my mind.*
> *Steady my hurried pace*
> *With a vision of eternal reach of time.*
> *Give me,*
> *Amidst the confusion of my day,*
> *The calmness of the everlasting hills.*
> *Break the tensions of my nerves*
> *With the soothing music of the singing streams*
> *That live in my memory.*
> *Help me to know*
> *The magical restoring power of sleep.*
> *Teach me the art*
> *Of taking minute vacations of slowing down*
> *to look at a flower;*
> *to chat with an old friend or make a new one;*
> *to pet a stray dog;*
> *to watch a spider build a web;*
> *to smile at a child;*
> *or to read a few lines from a good book.*
> *Remind me each day*
> *That the race is not always to the swift;*

That there is more to life than increasing its speed.
Let me look upward
Into the branches of the towering oak
And know that it grew great and strong
Because it grew slowly and well.
Slow me down, Lord,
And inspire me to send my roots deep
Into the soil of life's enduring values
That I may grow toward the stars
Of my greater destiny.[8]

—Orin L. Crain

2. Building and maintaining a strong relationship with your spouse. President Hinckley reminded his audience that despite all the emphasis we place on families, the husband-wife relationship is paramount—even ahead of the children. When that relationship is lacking, all other relationships—with God, with our children, with others—are adversely affected, and the opposite is true as well. When that primary relationship is strong, our other relationships and service are enriched. I am reminded of a story I once heard a colleague share. He told of taking their last child—the "baby" of the family—to the Missionary Training Center to report for his mission. When they returned to their home, his wife sat at the kitchen table and began to sob. This husband tried to comfort her. When the mother finally regained her composure she said to her husband, "You are all I have now!" To which he responded, "I'm all you've ever really had!" Children and grandchildren will come and go. In time, if they are faithful and righteous, they will be sealed to their own spouses for time and all eternity. But if we are wise and have our priorities straight, our spouse will be our eternal companion, our best friend—the most important earthly relationship!

3. Strengthening our families—immediate and extended. We are all familiar with the phrase that President David O. McKay was fond of quoting: "No other success can compensate for failure in the home."[9] In a similar vein, President Harold B. Lee reminded us that "the greatest of the Lord's work" that any of us will ever do "will be within the walls of [our] own homes."[10] Truly, our priorities are right when we focus our attention on eternal relationships and not so much on people or positions or things that are temporary and transitory, at best, or diverting and destructive at worst.

When I served as a bishop many years ago, I had impressed upon my mind a valuable lesson that gave much-needed perspective. In a meeting of the bishops of the stake, a wise leader reminded us that if we were to die that week, there would be a new bishop called and sustained in our wards within a matter of days or weeks. The ward would move on and would function quite well without us. "In fact," he said, "you can see how indispensable you are as bishop when you put your fist in a bucket of water and pull it out and see what hole is left." That hit me right between the eyes! He wanted us to understand that the hole left in our homes and in the lives of our families would be much wider and deeper than the one left in the ward. The vacancy in the bishop's office would be quickly (and, at least in my case, easily) filled. But the hole at home could never be adequately filled.

Each of us, whether we are married or not, is somebody's son or daughter, a brother or sister, perhaps even an aunt or an uncle. Those relationships are vital and matter more than we can imagine. The influence that is given and received within the family circle is more expansive than the value—both in fulfillment received and service rendered—of our jobs, hobbies, or even church callings. At a commencement ceremony at Vassar College, prominent physician, Dr. Bernadine Healy stated: "As a physician, who has been deeply privileged to share the most profound moments of people's lives including their final moments, let me tell you a secret. People facing death don't think about what degrees they have earned, what positions they have held, or how much wealth they have accumulated. At the end, what really matters is who you loved and who loved you."[11]

No wonder President McKay repeatedly reminded us about real success in life. More than just happiness and personal fulfillment in life, the efforts and service we render within the family are vital to our own spiritual progression and ultimate exaltation. Elder Dallin H. Oaks taught: "Now is the time for each of us to work toward our personal conversion, toward becoming what our Heavenly Father desires us to become. As we do so, we should remember that our family relationships—*even more than our Church callings*—are the setting in which the most important part of that development can occur. The conversion we must achieve requires us to be a good husband and father or a good wife and mother. *Being a successful Church leader is not enough.* Exaltation is an eternal family experience, and it is our mortal family experiences that are best suited to prepare us for it."[12]

Finally, President Hinckley reminded the Saints in that congregation, as well as each of us today, that we should have as one of our fundamental priorities:

4. Service in the Church. In light of his first three priorities, this fourth one may seem a little strange. But there is power and purpose in service in the kingdom. While much good can come from serving and helping others within the context of church callings, the real reason we should have this as a priority in our lives is that it can help us to know the Master better. He is that "good part" we should seek; and serving his flock enables us to know him. Service in the Church can strengthen our spirituality. Faithfulness in our callings can provide us with life-tutorials that cannot be obtained in any other way. Service in the Church, however, is a means to an end, not the end itself. The Savior is the end that we seek, and our service can pave the way. Yet, if we never come to realize the proper role and priority of service in the Lord's kingdom, we may end up like those of whom Jesus spoke: "Many will say to me in that day, Lord, Lord, have we not prophesied in thy name? and in thy name have cast out devils? and in thy name done many wonderful works?" (Matthew 7:22). We could interject, "Have we not been bishops, high councilors, Relief Society and Young Women presidents? Have we not organized great ward parties and produced the best road show ever? To which Jesus will say, "You have fulfilled callings, but you never came to know me!"

When we get any of these priorities "out of whack" or we intentionally or unwittingly mix up their proper sequence, we become "cumbered by much serving"—frustrated instead of fulfilled, harassed and harried rather than happy. When we are diverted and distracted and drawn in so many directions away from what matters most, our spiritual tanks are left empty. We are left depleted, depressed, and discouraged—all because our priorities got mixed up.[13]

PUTTING CHRIST AT THE CENTER OF OUR LIVES

Perhaps the most important phrase in the story of Mary and Martha and their interaction with the Master is this: *"One thing is needful."* Jesus gently and lovingly chided Martha for being "careful [worried] and troubled about many things" (Luke 10:41). The many things were not just worries about family or health or conditions in the world. An interesting translation of this passage reveals that the "things" which caused her so much consternation were, in reality, the many different dishes she had prepared for this dinner.[14] Jesus taught her that all of her elaborate preparations and the wide array of side dishes she had prepared for him and her guests were *nice, but not necessary.* She had done much more than the Savior required or even desired.

"Only one thing is needful," Jesus said to her. Remember the translation of the word *thing*—dish. Jesus is saying to her that a simple meal with only a few dishes—really only one—would have been ample. Martha was, in reality, wasting much time, energy, and resources. Worse yet, she seems to have lost perspective as to *why* she was having the dinner anyway. I can almost hear Martha saying what I have heard perhaps a million times in my own life: "But I want it to be really nice—something people will remember!"

Now, don't get me wrong. I believe that we should do things nicely—things that are appealing both to the eye and the taste buds, to the heart and the soul. But what was more important—to have a really nice dinner for the guests or to be able to spend time at the feet of the Savior, especially knowing that his days on earth were numbered? Can you see how Jesus must have felt? I can almost hear the Master saying, "*Martha, I want you to spend time with me, not spend all your time in the kitchen. Why are you upset with Mary when she is doing that which I wish you were doing as well—spending time with me!*"

Like the family dinner I described earlier—the one that creates chaos and causes stress to the point that we can't wait for the relatives to leave—we are Martha-like when our service focuses more on *what* we do than on *why* we do it. For example, several years ago when I was a Young Men president, I was often guilty of, *first,* helping the young men plan an activity that they really wanted to do, and only *then* scrambling to find a "priesthood purpose" for our activity. "Building quorum brotherhood" soon became the catch-all purpose for all of our activities. Whether it was playing basketball or waterskiing, we were "building quorum brotherhood." I still feel guilty for doing that—putting *plans* ahead of *purposes*, focusing on the *what we wanted to do* instead of the *why we should be doing it*.

One particular activity stands out in my memory these many years later. We had an impressive winter activity for the youth at Mutual Dell Lodge in American Fork canyon. The leaders had practically killed themselves getting everything ready and getting all the kids involved. I was the most popular guy there—because I brought the pizzas. Within a matter of minutes the pizza was devoured, the hot chocolate consumed, and the brownies were but a distant memory. I don't remember much else except that the youth scattered and the leaders spent the rest of the evening doing the required cleanup. I think that bothered me most of all, because it appeared to me that the youth viewed the Church as merely an activity outlet and the leaders as merely servants in providing them with fun and amusement.

As I drove down the canyon thinking of all the time and effort and the hundreds of dollars of sacred tithing funds that had been spent, I wondered if it had been worth it. We characterized the event as a success because the kids had fun, but was that really our purpose? One thought nagged me for a long, long time—we spent more money on that one youth activity than many wards and branches of the Church in other parts of the world have for their entire yearly budget. Don't get me wrong—it was fun, it was nice. And sometimes we do things in the Church that are merely for social purposes, and that is okay. But the question that I pondered after all of that was, "Was it all necessary?" *What was the real purpose for doing what we did?* Did that activity bring souls closer to Christ or did we hurry and scurry, plan and prepare, spend and clean, and worry and fret, only to discover that which was most important—even absolutely vital—had been missed?

I still see many of the priests that were in my quorum years ago. And do you know what? Not one of them has ever mentioned that activity! Yet they do remember and comment on other things—things that touched their lives and instilled faith and testimonies in their hearts—and those other things are usually simple things, not the elaborate or costly. And, the things these young men did mention as being memorable and influential most often took place in the classroom or at a simple, yet focused, activity or a meaningful service project where they saw the gospel in action and felt the Spirit of the Lord touching their hearts. The Lord has declared,

"Out of small things proceedeth that which is great" (D&C 64:33). Super-duper activities and "really nice" dinners may build memories, but the "virtue of the word of God" and the Spirit of the Lord build testimonies and instill spiritual strength to meet today's challenges.

When the Church announced its new budget policy many years ago, there were some expressions of concern. How will we ever be able to do everything for the youth and for the ward on such a small budget? How can we go on a "super-activity"? What will we have to cut out? The Brethren were mindful of those concerns. Perhaps they were trying to teach us that only "one thing is needful." At a fireside for the entire Church to discuss this new budget policy, President Boyd K. Packer taught: "Nothing essential will be lost; rather, essential things will be rediscovered, be found! . . . Sometimes *more* can be *less* and sometimes *less* is *more*."[15] Whether it be in our personal lives, in our homes, or in our service in the Church, perhaps we should remember Nephi's counsel in the Book of Mormon. He was quoting the prophet Isaiah when he declared: "Come, my brethren [and sisters], every one that thirsteth, come ye to the waters; and he that hath no money, come buy and eat; yea, come buy wine and milk without money and without price. Wherefore, do not spend money for that which is of no worth, nor your labor for that which cannot satisfy" (2 Nephi 9:50–51).

There is another phrase Jesus used as he taught Martha that has profound significance. When Martha expressed her frustration that her sister Mary was not helping her with the "many things" she was doing, she asked Jesus to scold Mary and make her help. That sounds like some of the sibling squabbles we have had at our house—"Mom, make her help! Dad, make him stop!" Wisely, Jesus did not give in to her, but instead lovingly taught an important lesson. We often think that Mary had not done anything to help. But that is not necessarily the case. She may have done her part and have made the necessary preparations, but reached a point when she thought *enough is enough—the time has come to be with the Master.* What Mary was doing was something, the Savior declared, *"which shall not be taken away from her"* (Luke 10:42; emphasis added). What did the Lord mean by that? The implication seems to be that the things Martha was worrying about and spending her time doing would be "taken from her." How could that be? The dinner—no matter how pleasing the preparations were and how delicious the food may have been—would soon be gone, forgotten, with nothing much to show for it (except perhaps a few extra pounds gained).

Mary, on the other hand, had been taught at the feet of the Savior. What she learned in her mind—what she felt in her heart, what she experienced in her soul—could not be taken away. Similarly, when we get bogged down in the "thick of thin things," when our efforts, preparations, activities—that which takes our time, energy, and money, no matter how noble our intentions— diverts or distracts us from that which should matter most, we will sense that we have lost something important. I love the imagery that Nephi uses in the Book of Mormon that perhaps applies to us modern-day Marthas (and Marvins). When we lose our spiritual focus, when we "look beyond the mark"—whether it be individual or institutional—we become like the man who Nephi says goes to bed hungry and thirsty and dreams that he eats and drinks until he is full, only to awake from his dream to discover that his soul is still empty (see 2 Nephi 27:3). That is why Jesus reminds us that some things do not satisfy the soul or have lasting impact; whereas, there is something that does. That one "needful thing"—that which cannot be taken away—is the Lord himself and his eternal gospel. As Nephi declared: "Come unto the Holy One of Israel, and feast upon that which perisheth not, neither can be corrupted, and let your soul delight in fatness" (2 Nephi 9:51). This leads to one last point concerning this story.

The key phrase in the scriptural account of Mary and Martha—the moral of the story if you will—seems to be *"[she] hath chosen that good part"* (Luke 10:42). Jesus is using a play on words here. The word *part* is sometimes rendered as "portion." Jesus is using the food and the dishes Martha has prepared as his object lesson. There is a double meaning in his words—"but one thing is needful." He is certainly telling Martha that a simple meal—"one thing," maybe even only one dish—would have sufficed for the occasion; but there is something else he is saying. There is something more needful, more important, more life-sustaining than just one dish at the meal, for even that will pass away. The "one thing" that is needful—"that good part"—is Christ himself, his atoning sacrifice, his teachings, his plan of salvation, his charity, his pure and perfect love for us. This is not just "that good part" but is indeed "the best part"—the only part that can never be taken away. No matter what else we do in life—what we choose, what we enjoy, or what we become—it will have been in vain if we don't fully choose the "good part," even this "best part," and take a heaping portion of it into our lives. Christ is the "Bread of Life" and the "Living Waters" that can nourish our souls and satisfy our spiritual hunger. Nothing else has that kind of power.

In recent years, President Gordon B. Hinckley has reminded us of our covenantal obligation to retain converts to the Church. He often says that it doesn't matter one whit if we baptize millions and yet do nothing to keep them safe and faithful in the gospel fold. He has said that all of us—new converts to the less active to lifetime members with pioneer ancestry who can trace their genealogy back past Adam—need three things to remain steadfast in these trying times. We need:

1. To be nourished by the good word of God.
2. A friend (social connections).
3. A responsibility.[16]

Each of these is important and vital. Yet real spiritual power, saving power, indeed, is to be found in the first one. Any person who does not get the spiritual nourishment the gospel affords will have shallow roots and will quickly wilt in the scorching heat of temptations and tribulations. That is why we must never lose sight of *why* we do what we do. All that we do in the Church, all that we do in our homes, all that we do in our personal lives should be leading us and those we love to him and to the partaking of his love, his mercy, and his salvation. Some things are interesting, other things are important, but one thing is absolutely imperative. He is "that good part." In fact, he is the "best part." Only in Christ is there to be found lasting sustenance. Without that "main dish," all other things are ultimately tasteless and unsatisfying. Only when we choose to partake of "that good part" are we able to know the abundance of life that Jesus offers (see John 10:10). As President Gordon B. Hinckley declared: "With all our doing, with all our leading, with all our teaching, the most important thing we can do for those whom we lead is to cultivate in their hearts a living, vital, vibrant testimony and knowledge of the Son of God, Jesus Christ, the Redeemer of the world, the Author of our salvation, He who atoned for the sins of the world and opened the way of salvation and eternal life. I would hope that in all we do we would somehow constantly nourish the testimony of our people concerning the Savior. I am satisfied, I know it's so, that whenever a man [or woman] has a true witness in his [or her] heart of the living reality of the Lord Jesus Christ all else will come together as it should. . . . That is the root from which all virtue springs among those who call themselves Latter-day Saints."[17]

Notes

1. See *Adam Clarke's Commentary on the Bible*, abridged by Ralph Earl (Kansas City: Beacon Hill Press, 1967; repr. Grand Rapids, Mich.: Baker Book House, n.d.), 872.

2. See John Knox, in *The Interpreter's Bible*, ed. George Arthur Buttrick, 12 vols. (New York: Abingdon Press, 1952), 8:197–98.

3. Neal A. Maxwell, *Notwithstanding My Weakness* (Salt Lake City: Deseret Book, 1981), 5.

4. Neal A. Maxwell, "Sharing Insights from My Life," BYU Devotional Address, 12 January 1999; in *Brigham Young University 1998–99 Speeches* (Provo: Brigham Young University, 1999), 113.

5. C. S. Lewis, *The Problem of Pain* (New York: Macmillan, 1962), 96.

6. M. Russell Ballard, "Be an Example of the Believers," *Ensign*, November 1991, 95.

7. William R. Bradford, "Unclutter Your Life," *Ensign*, May 1992, 28.

8. Orin L. Crain, "Slow Me Down, Lord," as cited in Dean L. Larsen, "The Peaceable Things of the Kingdom," *Brigham Young University 1984–85 Devotional and Fireside Speeches* (Provo: Brigham Young University Press, 1985), 71–72.

9. David O. McKay, in Conference Report, April 1935, 116.

10. Harold B. Lee, in Conference Report, April 1973, 130.

11. Bernadine Healy, "On Light and Worth: Lessons from Medicine," commencement address, Vassar College, 29 May 1994, 10, Special Collections; as quoted in Thomas S. Monson, "Dedication Day," *Ensign*, November 2000, 66.

12. Dallin H. Oaks, "The Challenge to Become," *Ensign*, November 2000, 33; emphasis added.

13. President Hinckley's four priorities were outlined by Jeffrey R. Holland 5 February 1999 at the Salt Lake Tabernacle in an address given to religious educators with the Church Educational System.

14. See Know, *Interpreter's Bible*, 8:197–98.

15. Boyd K. Packer, "Teach Them Correct Principles," *Ensign*, May 1990, 89–90; emphasis added.

16. Gordon B. Hinckley, in Conference Report, April 1997, 66.

17. Gordon B. Hinckley, *Teachings of Gordon B. Hinckley* (Salt Lake City: Deseret Book, 1997), 648.

CHAPTER 3

"IS IT I?"

Several years ago, while I was serving on a stake high council in Arizona, the stake president gave me a challenging assignment. We had encountered a problem in one of the wards in the stake. An individual in this ward had been sowing seeds of discord among the members through unwise words and actions. The stake president had asked several priesthood leaders to combine their efforts to solve the problem. As part of those efforts, he also asked me to speak in the ward. "You are to address the problem without specifically addressing the person," the president charged me. "Call the guilty person to repentance and teach the principles to the entire ward," he continued. "Be direct, but not too direct."

I struggled with the assignment. I prayed, studied, prepared, and prayed some more. Finally, the day to deliver my talk arrived. I had prepared with one particular person in mind, and as I presented my talk I envisioned myself giving the talk to that one person, as if we were the only two in the chapel. I felt that the Lord had indeed answered my prayers and blessed my efforts, for the Spirit was strong in the meeting and the desired message had been delivered—both from the pulpit and by the power of the Holy Ghost. At the conclusion of the meeting, a very interesting thing happened. The person who had been the "target" of my talk—the person who had been guilty of the contentious misbehavior that I had been addressing—approached me on the stand. I didn't know what to expect. Had I been too direct and forceful? Was the person offended? Was he going to express his displeasure to me (or punch me in the face)? Or had the Spirit touched him? Perhaps he was on his way to express to me his humble desire to repent and do better. Numerous thoughts of all the possibilities flashed through my mind. Within a moment, however, the true motivation for his visit to the stand became apparent, and I was left shaking my head in bewilderment.

"That was a great talk, Brother Top," he said. "You really hit the nail on the head! There could be no misunderstanding what you were saying. There was only one problem with it."

"What was that?" I asked, almost dreading to hear the answer.

"The problem was that Sister _____ was not here," he emphatically declared. "She really needed to hear your message. She has a problem with that, and you were speaking right to her. She needed to be here."

How could he have missed it? I was speaking directly to him, but all he could think about was how Sister _____ needed the message, not he. I have thought many times since that experience how common this character flaw is among us as mere mortals. It is the tendency of the natural man to deflect counsel and correction away from us and toward others. It is easy to look outward and see the weaknesses of others. It is painfully difficult to look deep within ourselves—at our weaknesses and our own need for change.

JUDGE NOT UNRIGHTEOUSLY

Jesus taught us to make our own hearts humbly receptive to corrective counsel and to avoid the natural tendency to judge, criticize, and condemn others when we are really the ones with the problem. In the Sermon on the Mount, the Master asked his disciples a probing question and then delivered a stinging rebuke:

"And why beholdest thou the mote that is in thy brother's eye, but considerest not the beam that is in thine own eye?

"Or how wilt thou say to thy brother, Let me pull out the mote out of thine eye; and, behold, a beam is in thine own eye?

"Thou hypocrite, first cast out the beam out of thine own eye; and then shalt thou see clearly to cast out the mote out of thy brother's eye" (Matthew 7:3–5).

It is clear that Jesus is using hyperbole to testify against one who is quick to point out the faults and failings of others and thus avoid self-examination. In the King James Version of the Bible, as translated from the Greek, the word *mote* can also be translated as *speck*—something as small as a tiny dust particle or other miniscule foreign object that irritates the eye. In contrast, the Greek term from which the word *beam* is translated connotes a large *log*, such as a building timber or construction beam. Can you see the humor in the use of these images? Just picture it in your own mind: a person with a steel construction beam sticking out of his own eye is overly concerned about a small speck of dust in his neighbor's eye. Yet we do the same thing when we deflect corrective counsel from ourselves and instead scornfully cast it upon others. This deflection, characterized by the Savior as "unrighteous judgment," occurs in myriad ways, yet almost always turns into gossip, backbiting, contention, and the loss of the Spirit.

The Savior's admonition, "Judge not, that ye be not judged" (Matthew 7:1) is often misinterpreted to mean that we should never make any judgments regarding people or situations. This is not what the Savior meant. The Lord expects us to be discerning and wise. We all need to make judgments every day. Sometimes our very lives—spiritual and physical—depend on those judgments. What, then, did Jesus mean, and how does his teaching apply to us?

To answer that question we must look at the meaning of the word *judge*. The Greek word from which *judge* is translated in this verse does not refer to the much-used definition, "to discern or to appraise something in order to make a wise decision." Its meaning is much harsher—it means *to condemn*. In this context, the word *judge* implies sentencing someone to death or prison. It connotes a sense of finality. What Jesus seems to be urging us to avoid is making value judgments about someone's spiritual standing with the Lord—assuming that someone is "unworthy" or is "unacceptable" before God—because of our own personal biases or misconceptions regarding the gospel standard. The natural man often condemns, criticizes, and gossips about a person for something of which he, himself, may be guilty. "Therefore thou art inexcusable, O man, whosoever thou art that judgest," the apostle Paul declared, "for wherein thou judgest another, thou condemnest thyself; for thou that judgest doest the same things" (Romans 2:1). Likewise, Jesus' teachings remind us that we have no right or stewardship to make a final judgment regarding the souls of men—only God can do that. While some have the calling and the keys to pass intermediate spiritual judgment on others, Jesus is reminding the rest of us that it is not our stewardship to make spiritual value statements regarding others' relationships with the Lord. To do so is unrighteous judgment, and it is always spiritually destructive—both to the *judge* and the *judged*.

I once received a paper from a student in one of my religion classes at BYU that sadly illustrated the destructive nature of unrighteous judgment. In analyzing the revelation regarding the three degrees of glory, as recorded in Doctrine and Covenants section 76, this young woman boldly declared that her father would inherit only the terrestrial kingdom. For the next several pages, she recounted all the ways that her father had "rejected" the gospel. I could sense a deep feeling of hurt on her part, but there was something more—something more dangerous. There was an underlying tone of anger and bitterness directed at her father for not joining the Church. It was clear that she had "written him off"—condemned him to terrestrial glory and "not one bit more!" I was so bothered by her judgmental sentiments that I wrote a few observations on her paper. I passed back the papers, and it couldn't have been much more than a nanosecond after she read my comments that she was in my office to "defend" herself. Once again she enumerated the many ways that her father had "rejected" the gospel. I listened politely. When I tried to explain that perhaps she didn't have at her disposal all of the information the Lord would need to make a perfect judgment in her father's case, she wouldn't hear of it. "He is going to the terrestrial kingdom, for it is right here in the scriptures!" she declared, pointing to her Doctrine and Covenants. The more I tried to dissuade her from passing such a final judgment on her loved one, the more upset she became. It was clear that she was deeply hurt by her father's irreligious attitude. Yet I sensed in some small way the hurt that her father must feel by her judgment. I could almost see him "digging in his heels" against her constant judgment and criticism of him. He would "show her" by not allowing the Spirit to touch his heart. There was a terrible strain in the relationship—caused not so much by the gospel, but rather by a daughter's unrighteous judgment and a father's stubborn reaction to it. Each was hurting the other, but both were left hurting themselves. Perhaps the daughter's appraisal of her father's spiritual condition will be borne out on the great Judgment Day. In the meantime, however, her unrighteous condemnation chased away any place for mercy, patience, and familial love and cooperation.

FORMS OF UNRIGHTEOUS JUDGMENT

Two forms of unrighteous judgment seem especially common in our society—judging by the traditions of men and judging with limited knowledge. The Savior's illustrations and prescriptive teachings are just as relevant to us today as they were for those disciples who sat at his feet upon the shore of the Sea of Galilee.

Judging by the Traditions of Men

On one occasion, the Savior declared, "Judge not according to the appearance, but judge righteous judgment" (John 7:24). Judging by appearance includes much more than just observing how a person may dress. It involves making unrighteous judgments—spiritual value statements—based on how things appear to us *outwardly,* not on how things "really are" (Jacob 4:13). The Joseph Smith Translation of this passage adds another important dimension: "Judge not according to *your traditions*" (JST John 7:24; emphasis added). The Jews of Jesus' day ascribed as much (and often more) authority to the practices and rituals passed down by the traditions of the Rabbis as they did to the commandments and teachings found in the holy scriptures. The Master rebuked them for the unrighteous judgments they made based on traditions that were not divine criteria for righteousness. For example, Jesus' disciples were condemned by the Pharisees for eating bread without washing their hands (see Mark 7:1–15). According to *tradition,* such an innocent oversight was tantamount to a capital offense.

The legal washing of the hands before eating was especially sacred to the Rabbinist; not to do so was a crime as great as eating the flesh of swine. Consider this passage from Cunningham Geikie, author of *The Life and Words of Christ:* "'He who neglects handwashing,' says the book Sohar, 'deserves to be punished here and hereafter.' 'He is to be destroyed out of the world, for in handwashing is contained the secret of the ten commandments.' . . . 'He who eats bread without hand-washing,' says Rabbi Jose, 'is as if he went in to a harlot.' The later Schulchan Aruch enumerates twenty-six rules for this rite in the morning alone. 'It is better to go four miles to water than to incur guilt by neglecting handwashing,' says the Talmud. 'He who does not wash his hands after eating,' it says, 'is as bad as a murderer.'"[1]

It is easy for us to look back at such traditions with smug curiosity and laugh about how silly they seem today. It is easy for us to see how ludicrous it is to spiritually equate failure to wash one's hands with adultery or murder—to spiritually condemn someone because of our cultural expectation. The problem is, however, that we often make the same judgments today, only with different traditions and cultural expectations.

We may place a cultural gospel—"The Gospel According to Popular Interpretation"—ahead of the real gospel. Sometimes we place higher expectations on others and ourselves because of our traditions, expectations, or faulty preconceptions of what the Lord desires of his disciples. For example, is a Relief Society teacher less spiritual or less acceptable to the Lord if she doesn't have a nice tablecloth and centerpiece as part of her lesson? Of course not! Yet, we sometimes unwittingly cause others to feel that way because of our unrighteous judgments. We occasionally look down our noses at those who may not do things exactly the way we do and/or expect others to do. Judging or condemning others on these grounds is as ludicrous (and hypocritical) as calling a person wicked for not washing his hands before a meal.

I was amused a few years ago when a recent convert shared with me an interesting observation. She said that she didn't feel accepted as a part of the sisters of the ward until she wore a denim jumper to church, just like the other sisters did. (In fact, in her early days in the Church she thought that it was actually a Relief Society requirement to dress a certain way and have a certain hairstyle. She was afraid that she wouldn't be able to go to the temple if she wasn't exactly like the other sisters.) Whether it was perceived or real I can't say; nonetheless, she felt judged by others if she didn't conform in appearance with others or abide by traditions or some arbitrary cultural requirement. President Brigham Young observed among the Saints in his day a similar tendency to criticize and condemn others because of outward appearances or cultural traditions.

"How I regret the ignorance of this people—how it floods my heart with sorrow to see so many Elders of Israel who wish everybody to come to their standard and be measured by their measure. Every man must be just so long, to fit their iron bedstead, or be cut off to the right length: if too short, he must be stretched, to fill the requirement.

"If they see an erring brother or sister, whose course does not comport with their particular idea of things, they conclude at once that he or she cannot be a Saint, and withdraw their fellowship, concluding that, if they are in the path of truth, others must have precisely their weight and dimensions."[2]

Judging with Limited Knowledge

How would you feel if you were to be judged by the Lord in the truest sense of the word—*condemned* or *sentenced* to an eternal fate—based on a small snippet of your life's story? That snippet might highlight one of your "bad days" and include nothing from your "good days." Such a narrow view would not yield a true picture of what you did with your life, what you are really like as a person, and what is really going on inside your head and heart. For us to be condemned without the "facts" would strip God of justice and mercy and make him a cruel and capricious tyrant. And, is that not what we become when we condemn and criticize others without the facts? Often we think we know, when in reality we see only a snippet—if that much! Several years ago my friend and BYU colleague, Art Bassett, shared an interesting story in the *Ensign* that illustrates this principle:

"[While teaching an institute class], I was troubled when one person whispered to another all through the opening prayer. The guilty parties were not hard to spot because they continued whispering all through the class. I kept glaring at them, hoping that they would take the hint, but they didn't seem to notice. Several times during the hour, I was tempted to ask them to take their conversation outside if they felt it was so urgent—but fortunately something kept me from giving vent to my feelings.

"After the class, one of them came to me and apologized that she hadn't explained to me before class that her friend was deaf.

The friend could read lips, but since I was discussing—as I often do—with my back to the class, writing on the chalkboard and talking over my shoulder, my student had been 'translating' for her friend, telling her what I was saying. To this day I am thankful that both of us were spared the embarrassment that might have occurred had I given vent to a judgment made without knowing the facts."[3]

One of my favorite hymns is "Lord, I Would Follow Thee." This verse speaks beautifully to this principle:

> *Who am I to judge another*
> *When I walk imperfectly?*
> *In the quiet heart is hidden*
> *Sorrow that the eye can't see.*
> *Who am I to judge another?*
> *Lord, I would follow thee.*[4]

The phrase, "In the quiet heart is hidden sorrow that the eye can't see," helps me recognize the spiritual shortsightedness of judging—condemning and criticizing (and often gossiping about)—someone when I neither know all the facts nor perceive the heart and intent of another. We seldom, if ever, know all the circumstances surrounding a person's life and the way he or she has chosen or is forced to live it. Perhaps the intents of the heart are much nobler than the behavior, which may be hampered by a lack of knowledge and understanding or by weaknesses yet to be overcome. It might be that the person is doing the best he or she can. Or it may simply be a matter of differences in spiritual progression among God's children. "If you are prone to criticize or judge," Elder H. Burke Peterson of the Seventy once taught, "remember, we never see the target a man aims at in life. We only see what he hits."[5]

Clearly, unrighteous judgment is the condemnation of another when we can't see the big picture (which only God can), when we criticize another without knowing all the circumstances in his or her life without perceiving the desires and intents of the heart. On the other hand, to "judge righteous judgment" is to give the person every benefit of the doubt, to not excuse what he or she does (if it is truly wrong or unrighteous) but to try to understand it. We must endeavor as best we can to "looketh on the heart" in judging others (1 Samuel 16:7). Elder Dallin H. Oaks demonstrated the importance of this principle in referring to the judgments we pass on one another and the labels that we often attach to our brothers and sisters in the Church.

"We tend to think of members in categories according to 'activity': active, less active, inactive, and so on. These categories are defined according to observable action, notably attendance at Church meetings. They take little or no account (positive or negative) of the things of the heart. This is a misleading omission.

"A person may love God with all his or her heart, might, mind, and strength, and still be in a circumstance in which it is impossible or extremely difficult to do the actions that are customarily judged to constitute 'activity.' . . .

"Even where a person is 'less active' because of carelessness or indifference, it is well to remember that the contrast between this member and some apparently active members may be quite different than meets the eye. Consider the contrast between deficiencies in actions and deficiencies in motives and attitudes. Who is more acceptable to God, a man who is indifferent to God and his fellowmen but attends church regularly to promote his business interests, or a man who loves God and his fellowmen but rarely attends meetings? Both of these men are missing blessings and growth. Both have need to change. But which is in a better position to bring himself in total harmony with God? Attendance patterns can be altered in an instant. A new resolve, proven by subsequent conduct, can repair inaction. But a defect of the heart is much more serious and requires far more time and effort to repair."[6]

When we judge someone unrighteously (remember, the word *judge* means "to condemn")—whether judging by some artificial and shallow standards such as appearance or traditions, or condemning someone when we really don't have all the facts—we exhibit what Elder Oaks characterized as "a defect of the heart." How then can we avoid such a spiritual sickness before it happens or cure this "heart disease" if we are afflicted? The teachings of Jesus and the examples of his true disciples provide the proper prescription.

THE NEED FOR PERSONAL INTROSPECTION

At the Last Supper, after Jesus had washed the feet of the apostles, he announced, "Ye are clean, but not all" (John 13:10). John then added this commentary: "For he knew who should betray him; therefore said he, Ye are not all clean" (John 13:11). The Gospel of Mark more explicitly states: "And as they sat and did eat, Jesus said, Verily I say unto you, One of you which eateth with me shall betray me" (Mark 14:18). I have often wondered what was going through the hearts and minds of the disciples when they heard this shocking announcement. They probably could have immediately pointed their fingers at Judas. I can almost hear the whispers in that upper room. "Of course it is Judas! You know how strange he's been acting." Perhaps others could have said, "Judas is surely the betrayer. He has had a chip on his shoulder ever since the Master taught at Capernaum" (see John 6:59–71). There could have been smug nods among them as they confidently identified Judas as the one and glared scornfully at him. Perhaps they could have justifiably condemned Judas and cast him from their midst. Yet, there was none of that. The scriptural account gives us a glimpse of true discipleship and the fruits of "righteous judgment." Mark records: "And they began to be sorrowful, and to say unto him *one by one, Is it I?*" (Mark 14:19; emphasis added).

There is a powerful lesson in that simple story. Although only three words, the phrase, "*Is it I?*" speaks volumes about true discipleship—about a humble follower of the Master who seeks to put off the natural man and its tendency to judge, condemn, and criticize others. Modern-day disciples must likewise ask themselves, *Is it I?* President Boyd K. Packer observed:

"We who have been called to lead the Church are ordinary men and women with ordinary capacities struggling to administer a church which grows at such a pace as to astound even those who watch it closely. Some are disposed to find fault with us; surely that is easy for them to do. *But they do not examine us more searchingly than we examine ourselves.*"[7]

"Meek introspection may yield some bold insights!"[8] Elder Neal A. Maxwell observed. One of the bold insights that will come with self-examination is a stark realization of the truth of the apostle Paul's words, "For all have sinned, and come short of the glory of God" (Romans 3:23). We all have our share of sins. We all need to repent. We all need the mercy of Christ. Such a bold insight makes it difficult to condemn others.

> *Who am I to judge another*
> *When I walk imperfectly?*

Through the years I have served in a variety of leadership callings in the Church. In many of these assignments I have had responsibilities to sit on disciplinary councils and to serve as a judge in Israel. It is always sobering. One of the by-products, however, of such serious responsibilities is that it forces me to examine my own worthiness to pass judgments. Often the Spirit reminds me that, although I may not be guilty of the transgression that the person who sits before me carries, I have my share of sins and weaknesses that need attention. I am constantly reminded of my need for strength and guidance that comes from the Lord and the continual need for his mercy. Each time I ask the temple recommend questions, I am reminded of the "Is it I?" account in the New Testament. As I verbally ask the person sitting across from me—

- Do *you* have a firm testimony of the restored gospel?
- Do *you* earnestly strive to do your duty in the Church?
- Are *you* honest in your dealings with your fellowmen?
- Do *you* keep the covenants you have made?

—I think of the apostles at the Last Supper and mentally replace the word *you* with *I*.

When we hear exhortations from the pulpit or receive corrective counsel, we should remember, as the Savior taught and exemplified, the natural man *deflects to others* and a true disciple *reflects on self*. When we are tempted to judge another—to judge unrighteously without knowing all the facts—it would be well for us to ask, "Lord, is it I?"

Do I know the facts? Do I really know all the circumstances? Do I know what the person was thinking and feeling? Do I know his heart?

Am I guiltless? Am I casting stones that could also be directed at me? How am I doing at overcoming my own weaknesses?

Would I be considerably better or act dramatically different if I faced the same temptations and challenges or experienced the same circumstances?

How do I want others to judge me? How do I want the Lord to judge me?

In warning against passing unrighteous judgment on others, the Savior taught a principle that I like to call "The Doctrine of Reciprocity." In modern-day vernacular it would say, "What goes around comes around!"

"Judge not unrighteously, that ye be not judged: but judge righteous judgment. *For with what judgment ye judge, ye shall be judged:*

and with what measure ye mete, it shall be measured to you again" (JST Matthew 7:1–2; emphasis added).

It is sobering to think that I will be judged in like manner to the way I have judged others. If I want to have the Lord judge me not only with justice, but also with mercy, then I must do the same in my judgments of others. In fact, the more I apply the "Is it I?" principle to myself, the less room there will be in my heart for judging others.

"Examine yourselves," the apostle Paul admonished, "whether ye be in the faith; prove your own selves" (2 Corinthians 13:5). The more I focus on my own shortcomings, the less room in my peripheral vision I will have to criticize and condemn my fellow-men. As we strive to become true disciples of the Perfect Judge, we can learn to "judge righteously" if we will narrow our view— looking *inward* instead of *outward*. If we continually ask "Is it I?" we will come to a stark realization. "Search your hearts, and see if you are like God," the Prophet Joseph Smith declared. "I have searched mine, and feel to repent of all my sins."[9]

Notes

1. Cunningham Geikie, as quoted by Bruce R. McConkie in *The Mortal Messiah: From Bethlehem to Calvary*, 4 vols. (Salt Lake City: Deseret Book, 1979–81), 2:400–401.

2. Brigham Young, *Journal of Discourses*, 26 vols. (London: Latter-day Saints Book Depot, 1854–86), 8:9.

3. Arthur R. Bassett, "Floods, Winds, and the Gates of Hell," *Ensign*, June 1991, 8.

4. Susan Evans McCloud, "Lord, I Would Follow Thee," *Hymns of The Church of Jesus Christ of Latter-day Saints* (Salt Lake City: The Church of Jesus Christ of Latter-day Saints, 1985), no. 220; emphasis added. Used with permission.

5. H. Burke Peterson, "Removing the Poison of an Unforgiving Spirit," *Ensign*, November 1983, 60.

6. Dallin H. Oaks, *Pure in Heart* (Salt Lake City: Bookcraft, 1988), 31–32.

7. Boyd K. Packer, "Revelation in a Changing World," *Ensign*, November 1989, 16.

8. Neal A. Maxwell, " 'Swallowed Up in the Will of the Father,'" *Ensign*, November 1995, 24.

9. Joseph Smith, *Teachings of the Prophet Joseph Smith*, sel. Joseph Fielding Smith (Salt Lake City: Deseret Book, 1972), 216.

CHAPTER 4

THE UNMERCIFUL
SERVANT

Just after I concluded my "Know Your Religion" lecture and began gathering up my papers, a woman approached the stand and said, "Brother Top, may I speak with you for a moment?" That "moment" quickly became more than an hour. Her husband had left her several years earlier for a younger woman. The marriage was ruined, the children devastated, and the contented and peaceful home that once prevailed was left in shambles. Because I had never experienced anything closely related to the trials she was enduring, it was only in a very small way that I could feel her pain. Nonetheless, my heart went out to her.

Through her tears, she expressed deep-seated anger at her husband for the pain he had purposely caused her and the children. In addition to her expressions of heartbreak and anger—which I felt were not only quite normal but also justifiable—she seethed with deep resentment. "I can never forgive him," she emphatically and repeatedly declared. "I can't believe they allowed him back in the Church," she stated. "It isn't fair that he should be able to go to the temple now." Over the next several minutes she explained to me that her ex-husband had been excommunicated for his adultery. After their divorce, he had later remarried and had become active again in the Church. After several years he had been rebaptized and ultimately (after another year or more) had his priesthood and temple blessings restored. It was like rubbing salt in the wound of this estranged wife. She was especially hurt and angry that her "cheating ex-husband" was now being allowed to be sealed to his new wife.

"Maybe he has repented and the Lord has forgiven him," I timidly suggested. It was as if a horse had kicked her in the stomach. "The Lord wouldn't forgive him, would he?" she asked, her eyes almost pleading that such forgiveness be beyond her ex-husband's reach. "If he really has repented, of course, the Lord can forgive even such a terrible sin as that," I stated. "That is the greatness of the Atonement." She shook her head and as she walked away she said, "Well, maybe the Lord can forgive him, but I don't know if I can."

I am sure that I did not understand what this good sister went through, nor did I feel what she had felt. I could, however, sense the mighty struggle that such forgiveness would require. She and I both knew that it is a commandment of God to forgive. The scriptures are full of such admonitions—but none of them say it will be easy.

"For if ye forgive men their trespasses, your heavenly Father will also forgive you," the Savior taught in the Sermon on the Mount. "But if ye forgive not men their trespasses, neither will your Father forgive your trespasses" (Matthew 6:14–15). In the Lord's Prayer, Jesus taught this concept by example as he prayed, "Forgive us our debts, as we forgive our debtors" (Matthew 6:12). And in our own dispensation, he declared: "I, the Lord, will forgive whom I will forgive, but of you it is required to forgive all men" (D&C 64:10). This is no arbitrary "do it because I say so" commandment. Like all commandments of God, it is designed not only to lead to our ultimate exaltation but also to bring us peace and happiness right here and now. "Whatever God requires is right, no matter what it is," the Prophet Joseph Smith declared, "although we may not see the reason thereof till long after the events transpire.

". . . But in obedience there is joy and peace unspotted, unalloyed; and as God has designed our happiness—and the happiness of all His creatures, He never has—He never will institute an

ordinance or give a commandment to His people that is not calcu-
lated in its nature to promote that happiness which He has designed,
and which will not end in the greatest amount of good and glory to
those who become the recipients of his law and ordinances."[1]

Certainly the commandment to forgive others is designed to
promote happiness and good in our lives here on earth and is
directly related to the glory that can be ours in the world to come.
The Savior repeatedly taught, both by precept and example, the
important relationship between our forgiving others and the Lord
forgiving us. Both types of forgiveness have much to do with our
earthly happiness and spiritual development. On one occasion the
Savior dramatically illustrated how this "Doctrine of Reciprocity"—*what you give is what you get*—is directly linked to our willingness to forgive others. It is found in a unique parable that has
come to be known as the parable of the unmerciful servant.

It was this question from Peter that elicited the Savior's teaching: "Lord, how oft shall my brother sin against me, and I forgive
him? till seven times?" (Matthew 18:21). It is evident from Peter's
question that he had a limited understanding of the higher law of
forgiveness. This deficiency, to a large degree, was due to the
Mosaic law's teaching of "an eye for an eye" retribution. Peter's
follow-up question, "Till seven times?" was intended to be a generous gesture, going far beyond the requirements of the ancient law.
Jesus, however, taught a still higher law when he responded, "I say
not unto thee, Until seven times: but, Until seventy times seven"
(Matthew 18:22). I do not believe Jesus was saying that we must
forgive only 490 times and on the 491st offense "all heck can break
loose."

"Therefore is the kingdom of heaven likened unto a certain
king, which would take account of his servants.

"And when he had begun to reckon, one was brought unto
him, which owed him ten thousand talents.

"But forasmuch as he had not to pay, his lord commanded him

to be sold, and his wife, and children, and all that he had, and payment to be made.

"The servant therefore fell down, and worshipped him, saying, Lord, have patience with me, and I will pay thee all.

"Then the lord of that servant was moved with compassion, and loosed him, and forgave him the debt.

"But the same servant went out, and found one of his fellowservants, which owed him an hundred pence: and he laid hands on him, and took him by the throat, saying, Pay me that thou owest.

"And his fellowservant fell down at his feet, and besought him, saying, Have patience with me, and I will pay thee all.

"And he would not: but went and cast him into prison, till he should pay the debt.

"So when his fellowservants saw what was done, they were very sorry, and came and told unto their lord all that was done.

"Then his lord, after that he had called him, said unto him, O thou wicked servant, I forgave thee all that debt, because thou desiredst me:

"Shouldest not thou also have had compassion on thy fellowservant, even as I had pity on thee?

"And his lord was wroth, and delivered him to the tormentors, till he should pay all that was due unto him.

"So likewise shall my heavenly Father do also unto you, if ye *from your hearts* forgive not every one his brother their trespasses" (Matthew 18:23–35; emphasis added).

The principle Jesus teaches with this parable is further highlighted with a broadened understanding of the relative value of the ancient monetary system. A talent was equivalent to approximately sixty minas. One mina was equivalent to one hundred denarii or pence. This means that the first servant was 600,000 times more indebted than his fellow servant, whom he cast into prison for a paltry debt of one hundred pence. In our culture, it would be like having the first servant be absolved—totally forgiven—of a 10-million-dollar debt, but then repossessing all the belongings of and imprisoning for fraud someone who is unable to repay a ten-dollar debt. Once again, Jesus uses hyperbole to expose the hypocrisy of petitioning the Lord to forgive our sins—which are oftentimes weighty and grievous—while we withhold mercy and forgiveness from others whose offenses against us may be small or even petty in comparison.

Even when the sins against us are much more than petty offenses or insignificant indiscretions, even when we have been deeply wounded and our hearts have been broken by the abominable actions of others, the Lord requires us to forgive. There is no getting around that commandment. If we withhold our forgiveness of others we stand "condemned before the Lord; for there remaineth in [us] *the greater sin*" (D&C 64:9; emphasis added). How is it that we would stand condemned? In what way would the greater sin be upon our heads?

FORGIVENESS AND THE ATONEMENT OF CHRIST

Each of us is dependent upon the Savior and his mercy to cleanse us from our sins, to work a "mighty change" in our hearts, and to help us to develop the divine nature that will enable us to return to God's presence. When we exercise faith in his purifying power we are able to make claim upon the tender mercy and divine forgiveness of the Lord. If we, however, refuse to forgive others, even as we are calling upon God to forgive us, we stand "condemned"—unforgiven of the Lord—because we have not yet experienced the change of heart that characterizes true repentance. Could it be that "the greater sin" remains with us because our unforgiving spirit reflects a desire on our part to deny or withhold the spiritual healing effects of the Atonement in the lives of others? Is not our stubborn refusal to extend mercy to others a subtle but real rejection of the Redeemer and his redemptive role in the lives of others as well as in our own? Can you see the hypocrisy Jesus is decrying in the parable of the unmerciful servant? It would be like uttering words such as these in a prayer: "Heavenly Father, please forgive me of my sins and please extend to me your patience, love, compassion, and mercy, *but* please don't forgive _____ because he isn't worthy of your mercy, love, and forgiveness!" Such a selfish and unmerciful attitude is almost Lucifer-like in that we desire to suppress the spiritual development of another and keep him chained in the bonds of sin. Refusing to forgive those who have offended us is assuming the right of judgeship to which we have no claim. Only Jesus—the Perfect Judge—has the right to condemn others and dispense prescriptions of punishment or the medicine of mercy. Attempting to usurp Christ's right to judge reflects a lack of faith in the justice of God and a reluctance on our part to allow the Savior, in his divine role, to "balance the books."

The "moral of the story" in the parable of the unmerciful servant is unmistakable: "If you don't forgive others, you won't be forgiven!" When it comes to forgiving others, the Savior doesn't seem to be giving us much "wiggle room." No matter how horribly we have been harmed, no matter how painful it may be, no matter how impossible it may seem, the commandment stands: "I, the Lord, will forgive whom I will forgive, but of you it is required to forgive all men" (D&C 64:10). To fail to do so is akin to denying the Atonement in the lives of others—and *that* is "the greater sin." As the great Christian scholar C. S. Lewis insightfully observed:

"We believe that God forgives us our sins; but also that He will not do so unless we forgive other people their sins against us. There is no doubt about the second part of this statement. It is in the Lord's Prayer; it was emphatically stated by our Lord. If you don't forgive you will not be forgiven. No part of His teaching is clearer, *and there are no exceptions to it*. He doesn't say that we are to forgive other people's sins provided they are not too frightful, or provided there are extenuating circumstances, or anything of that sort. *We are to forgive them all, however spiteful, however mean, how-ever often they are repeated. If we don't we shall be forgiven none of our own. . . .*

"We are offered forgiveness on no other terms. *To refuse it is to refuse God's mercy for ourselves.* There is no hint of exceptions and God means what He says."[2]

An Unwillingness to Forgive Cankers the Soul

The truth of the matter is that no attempt on our part, whether through our actions or our feelings, can have any impact on the role of the Atonement in the lives of others. Our failure to forgive will not necessarily prevent others from repenting or pre-clude them from partaking of the fruit of the tree of life—which is the love and mercy of Christ. We can condemn only ourselves. We can prevent only ourselves from tasting of the tree "whose fruit was desirable to make one happy" (1 Nephi 8:10). While we simmer and stew about the sins and souls of others, the effects of *our own sins* remain with us—we cannot be sanctified—and *our own souls* become poisoned with the toxin of bitterness and the venom of vengeance. Bishop H. Burke Peterson illustrated this principle with the following true story:

"Some years ago a group of teenagers from the local high school went on an all-day picnic into the desert on the outskirts of Phoenix. . . . The desert foliage is rather sparse—mostly mesquite, catclaw, and palo verde trees, with a few cactus scattered here and there. In the heat of the summer, where there are thickets of this desert growth, you may also find rattlesnakes as unwelcome residents. These young people were picnicking and playing, and during their frolicking, one of the girls was bitten on the ankle by a rattlesnake. As is the case with such a bite, the rattler's fangs released venom almost immediately into her bloodstream.

"This very moment was a time of critical decision. They could immediately begin to extract the poison from her leg, or they could search out the snake and destroy it. Their decision made, the girl and her young friends pursued the snake. It slipped quickly into the undergrowth and avoided them for fifteen or twenty minutes. Finally, they found it, and rocks and stones soon avenged the infliction.

"Then they remembered: their companion had been bitten! They became aware of her discomfort, as by now the venom had had time to move from the surface of the skin into the tissues of her foot and leg. Within another thirty minutes they were at the emergency room of the hospital. By then the venom was well into its work of destruction.

"A couple of days later I was informed of the incident and was asked by some of the young members of the Church to visit their friend in the hospital. As I entered her room, I saw a pathetic sight. Her foot and leg were elevated—swollen almost beyond recognition. The tissue in her limb had been destroyed by the poison, and a few days later it was found her leg would have to be amputated below the knee.

"It was a senseless sacrifice, the price of revenge. How much better it would have been if, after the young woman had been bitten, there had been an extraction of the venom from the leg in a process known to all desert dwellers."[3]

All too often we become "victims," like this snake-bitten young lady. The most painful wounds to our minds, hearts, and souls are usually self-inflicted. As victims of self-inflicted suffering, we become tormented not so much by the offenses against us as by our own unforgiving thoughts and attitudes. This suffering is, as Elder Boyd K. Packer characterized, "unnecessary suffering." Furthermore, if we do not get rid of these burdensome feelings in our hearts, our "self-inflicted penalties soon become cruel and unusual punishment."[4]

All too often we fall into the unfortunate condition of condemning the unforgiving and spiteful hearts around us while failing to recognize those same symptoms in ourselves. "We are all prone to brood on the evil done us," President Gordon B. Hinckley stated. "That brooding becomes a gnawing and destructive canker. . . . There is no peace in the nursing of a grudge. There is no happiness in living for the day when you can 'get even.'"[5] President Hinckley has also cited an interesting example from literature that poignantly portrays how such brooding and bitterness can actually serve to destroy one's own soul. The French writer Guy de Maupassant wrote of a peasant man named Hauchecome who had come to the village on market day to buy some goods.

"While walking through the public square, his eye caught sight of a piece of string lying on the cobblestones. He picked it up and put it in his pocket. His actions were observed by the village harness maker with whom he had previously had a dispute.

"Later in the day the loss of a purse was reported. Hauchecome was arrested on the accusation of the harness maker. He was taken before the mayor, to whom he protested his innocence, showing the piece of string that he had picked up. But he was not believed and was laughed at.

"The next day the purse was found, and Hauchecome was absolved of any wrongdoing. But, resentful of the indignity he had suffered because of the false accusation, he became embittered and would not let the matter die. Unwilling to forgive and forget, he thought and talked of little else. He neglected his farm. Everywhere he went, everyone he met had to be told of the injustice. By day and by night he brooded over it. Obsessed with his grievance, he became desperately ill and died. In the delirium of his death struggles, he repeatedly murmured, 'A piece of string, a piece of string.'"[6]

The sad demise of Hauchecome may be only a fictional account, but it certainly could represent the very real spiritual decline of many people. Each of us knows of friends or family members who have slowly destroyed themselves spiritually and emotionally by harboring bitterness and resentment. The examples often attest to the truth of the adage, "For the man with no forgiveness in his heart, life is worse than death."

While many who are unforgiving may not suffer total self-destruction, their spiritual progress can still become stymied to one degree or another. It may start as a simple grudge, but gradually and almost imperceptibly it can cause a serious shrinkage of the soul. Some thoughtful person once said, "Forgiving makes us free for giving." The opposite is also true. *When we fail to forgive, we fail to give.* It becomes increasingly more difficult for us to reach beyond ourselves because we become more self-centered and more focused on our own hurts rather than on healing the hurts of others. This in turn prevents us from obtaining the joy, blessings, and spiritual growth that come from service. Thus we find ourselves in a vicious downward cycle that we can break only by freeing ourselves from the ties of bitterness that bind us ever tighter. No wonder Jesus often taught of the importance of forgiving others. We know it is a true doctrine—for the Savior clearly taught it—but the question is not "Should I forgive?" but rather "How can I forgive?" The teachings of the Master provide us with answers to that question as well.

APPLYING THE HEART-HEALING BALM OF GILEAD

Our ability to forgive others who have trespassed against us may be our most difficult and demanding test of true discipleship—even when we have experienced marvelous spiritual manifestations in our lives, even when we possess unshakable testimonies of the truthfulness of the gospel.

Several years ago, after I had given a lecture on the subject of forgiving others, a woman approached me with a crucial question: "What can I do to rid myself of the terrible feelings and hatred I have in my heart for someone who deeply hurt and betrayed me?" I tried as well as I could to explain what the scriptures taught, but she was not satisfied with my answer. She seemed to be seeking some quick fix or self-help program for forgiving others— *Forgiveness Made Easy*. She had, as she explained, "tried so many things," but the bitterness in her heart remained. The longer we talked, the more I realized that she had not understood that it was *impossible* for her to forgive and cleanse her heart of all bitterness *all by herself*. She failed to see that we overcome the natural man not only by our own efforts to forgive and forget but also, and more important, through the atonement of Jesus Christ.

In ancient times a major export to Tyre and Egypt was an ointment made from the aromatic gum of resin-producing shrubbery in the Gilead region in the Holy Land. This "balm of Gilead" was renowned throughout the ancient Near East for its soothing and healing properties. Even today the phrase *balm of Gilead* symbolizes a spiritual power that can soothe the soul and heal the heart.

> *There is a Balm in Gilead,*
> *To make the wounded whole.*
> *There is a Balm in Gilead*
> *To heal the sin sick soul.*[7]

Both symbolically and literally, the afflicted person must make a generous application of the ointment to his own wounds to experience the promised healing. While each of us must do certain things to "apply" the balm of Gilead, the actual healing of the heart comes *only* from the Lord.

A gripping story from the life of Corrie ten Boom beautifully illustrates the twofold nature of forgiving others. Corrie, a Christian woman living in Holland, was arrested by the Nazi Gestapo for hiding Dutch Jews during World War II. She was sent to a concentration camp, and her remarkable story of faith and survival in the death camps is recounted in the book *The Hiding Place*. Years after the war and her liberation from the concentration camps she went to Germany to speak to congregations and to testify of the loving and forgiving nature of God. It was at one of these meetings where her Christian character and professed belief in forgiveness were ultimately tested.

"It was in a church in Munich that I saw him—a balding, heavyset man in a gray overcoat, a brown felt hat clutched between his hands. People were filing out of the basement room where I had just spoken, moving along the rows of wooden chairs to the door at the rear. It was 1947 and I had come from Holland to defeated Germany with a message that God forgives.

"It was the truth they needed most to hear in that bitter, bombed-out land, and I gave them my favorite mental picture. Maybe because the sea is not far from a Hollander's mind, I liked to think that that's where forgiven sins were thrown. 'When we confess our sins,' I said, 'God casts them into the deepest ocean, gone forever. . . .'

"The solemn faces stared back at me, not quite daring to believe. There were never questions after a talk in Germany in 1947. People stood up in silence, in silence collected their wraps, in silence left the room.

"And that's when I saw him, working his way forward against the others. One moment I saw the overcoat and brown hat; the next, a blue uniform and visored cap with its skull and crossbones. It came back with a rush: the huge room with its harsh overhead lights; the pathetic pile of dresses and shoes in the center of the floor; the shame of walking naked past this man. I could see my frail sister's form ahead of me, ribs sharp beneath the parchment skin. *Betsie, how thin you were!*

["Betsie and I had been arrested for concealing Jews in our home during the Nazi occupation of Holland; this man had been a guard at Ravensbruck concentration camp where we were sent.]

"Now he was in front of me, hand thrust out: 'A fine message, Fräulein! How good it is to know that, as you say, our sins are at the bottom of the sea.'

"And I, who had spoken so glibly of forgiveness, fumbled in my pocketbook rather than take that hand. He would not remember me, of course—how could he remember one prisoner among those thousands of women?

"But I remembered him and the leather crop swinging from his belt. I was face to face with one of my captors, and my blood seemed to freeze.

"'You mentioned Ravensbruck in your talk,' he was saying. 'I was a guard there.' No, he did not remember me.

"'But since that time,' he went on, 'I have become a Christian. I know that God has forgiven me for the cruel things I did there, but I would like to hear it from your lips as well. Fräulein,'—again the hand came out—'will you forgive me?'

"And I stood there—I whose sins had again and again to be forgiven—and could not forgive. Betsie had died in that place—could he erase her slow terrible death simply for the asking?

"It could not have been many seconds he stood there—hand held out—but to me it seemed hours as I wrestled with the most difficult thing I had ever had to do.

"For I had to do it—I knew that. The message that God forgives has a prior condition: that we forgive those who have injured us. 'If you do not forgive men their trespasses,' Jesus says, 'neither will your Father in heaven forgive your trespasses.'

"I knew it not only as a commandment of God, but as daily experience. Since the end of the war I had had a home in Holland for victims of Nazi brutality. Those who were able to forgive their former enemies were able to return to the outside world and rebuild their lives, no matter what the physical scars. Those who nursed their bitterness remained invalids. It was as simple and horrible as that.

"And I stood there with coldness clutching my heart. But forgiveness is not an emotion—I knew that too. Forgiveness is an act of the will, and the will can function regardless of the temperature of the heart. 'Jesus, help!' I prayed silently. 'I can lift my hand. I can do that much. You supply the feeling.'

"And so woodenly, mechanically, I thrust my hand into the one stretched out to me. And as I did, an incredible thing took place. The current started in my shoulder, raced down my arm, sprang into our joined hands. And then this healing warmth seemed to flood my whole being, bringing tears to my eyes.

"'I forgive you, brother!' I cried. 'With all my heart!'

"For a long moment we grasped each other's hands, the former guard and the former prisoner. I had never known God's love so intensely as I did then."[8]

Just as Corrie ten Boom was able to experience the God-given warmth of forgiveness *only after* she supplied the forgiving hand-shake, we too must be willing to perform certain volitional acts of forgiveness in order for God to "supply the feeling." May I suggest four things, as taught and exemplified by the Savior, we can do in order that God can endow us with the spirit of forgiveness, love, and peace.

"Leave It Alone"

The Chinese philosopher Confucius is reported to have taught: "To be wronged or robbed is nothing unless you continue to remember it." All too often we cling tenaciously to our griev-ances against those who have wronged us—mulling them over and over in our minds. Until we are willing to "let go" of our spiteful thoughts and emotions, we remain bound by our own self-imposed shackles of bitterness. We become like some small animals, such as monkeys or raccoons, that are easily trapped by a simple box with a hole in it just large enough for the animal to reach in and retrieve a morsel of food or a curious object. The hole, however, is too small to allow a fist formed by clinging to the object to come out again. The animal, unwilling to let go of the bait, is thus trapped.

The ideal attitude, "forgive and forget," may seem unrealistic, if not impossible to achieve. Each of us will cognitively remember how we have been wronged or injured, but we can indeed "forget" in the sense that we can conscientiously commit or covenant to "let go" of our hard feelings. We can determine to dwell no longer on the wrongs done us. We can force thoughts of retribution out of our minds. "Leave it alone," Elder Boyd K. Packer counseled.

"Some frustrations we must endure without really solving the problem. Some things that ought to be put in order are not put in order because we cannot control them. Things we cannot solve, we must survive. . . .

"If you brood constantly over a loss or a past mistake, look ahead—settle it.

"We call that forgiveness. Forgiveness is powerful spiritual medicine."[9]

This "leaving alone" of deeds that are done and cannot be undone and of circumstances that are beyond our control is the first step in "supplying the action"—preparing our hearts—so that God can "supply the feeling"—heal our hearts of hatred and bitterness.

"Pray for Them Which Despitefully Use You"

In the Sermon on the Mount, Jesus not only commanded his disciples to forgive others, but also gave them the means whereby that could be accomplished.

"Ye have heard that it hath been said, Thou shalt love thy neighbour, and hate thine enemy.

"But I say unto you, *Love* your enemies, *bless* them that curse you, *do good* to them that hate you, and *pray* for them which despitefully use you, and persecute you" (Matthew 5:43–44; emphasis added).

Often the question arises, "How can I love my enemies or forgive those who have hurt me when I have no feelings of affection for them or when I actually dislike them?" The Savior's celestial charge is based not on emotion but on volition. The words he used—*love, bless, pray*—imply *actions we choose to do* rather than feelings we naturally feel. Just as "letting go" involves a conscientious commitment on our part, so does this second prescript.

Several years ago I had an experience that taught me the profound yet practical meaning of Jesus' admonition to "pray for them which despitefully use you and persecute you." While sitting with a group of religious educators on the Mount of Beatitudes overlooking the Sea of Galilee, I asked each member of the group to share personal insights regarding the Sermon on the Mount. Most of the comments dealt with doctrinal points, but one member of the group who was serving as a bishop at the time shared an experience that taught all of us the timelessness and practicability of Jesus' simple teachings. He explained how he had counseled with a couple who were experiencing serious marital difficulties. There seemed to be little if any progress toward reconciliation. They had participated in professional counseling along with frequent and regular visits with the bishop. Nothing seemed to help. The couple was drifting further and further apart. Just when the bishop was most discouraged and felt that the marriage could not be saved, he thought of Jesus' admonition to "pray for your enemies." He had never before thought of that passage in a marriage or family context. As he pondered, it was clear to him that the Master's words had just as much, if not more, meaning for a failing marriage as the many other settings that we most often consider.

"I want each of you to pray for the other," the bishop counseled the couple. "Not just rote, empty prayers, but a real heartfelt prayer. I want you to plead with the Lord to bless and help your partner." The couple was somewhat stunned by the bishop's counsel, but they agreed to give it a try. As they left the bishop's office, he reminded them: "Now this isn't just a one-time thing. I want you to sincerely pray for your spouse every day. We'll talk again in a month."

At the end of the month, the couple returned to the bishop's office holding hands. All of their problems were not solved, but there was a spirit of love, kindness, and forgiveness that had long been absent in their marriage. "It's pretty hard to be angry at some-one for very long when you are earnestly praying for their well-being and blessing," the husband happily reported. Here was a living example—a walking, talking object lesson—that testified of the healing power of praying for our enemies.

The more we extend our compassion and charity to others—including our enemies—through heartfelt prayer, the more our icy feelings of hatred and resentment will melt away. When we unselfishly and mercifully pray for those who have offended us, we can in turn come confidently before our Father and petition in our own behalf.

"Do Good to Them That Hate You"

President Brigham Young often taught the Saints that sincere prayer must be accompanied by some action or commitment on our part. We must *do* something, not just *say* something. It is cer-tainly this principle that Jesus taught when he commanded, "Love your enemies, bless them that curse you, do good to them that hate you." Just as praying for someone who has hurt us has the poten-tial to soften our hearts, so too does doing something good—something kind, something beneficial—even if the person "hates" us or is unresponsive to our gestures of goodwill. These acts of doing good to those who have offended us—whether in a serious or simple manner—need not be some magnanimous gesture. We can, however, exercise simple sentiments of spiritual concern and Christlike compassion. Loving and forgiving our enemies—"doing good to them that hate you"—may not involve liking them or their deeds, but it must involve a commitment to "clothe [ourselves] with the bond of charity" (D&C 88:125). "We must try to feel about the enemy as we feel about ourselves," observed C. S. Lewis, "to wish that he were not bad, to hope that he may, in this world or another, be cured: in fact, to wish his good. . . . The rule for all of us is perfectly simple. Do not waste your time bothering whether you 'love' your neighbour; act as if you did. As soon as we do this we find one of the great secrets. When you are behaving as if you loved someone, you will presently come to love him. . . . If you do him a good turn, you will find yourself disliking him less. . . .

"The difference between a Christian and worldly man is not that the worldly man has only affections or 'likings' and the Christian has only 'charity.' The worldly man treats certain people kindly because he 'likes' them: the Christian, trying to treat every one kindly, finds himself liking more and more people as he goes on—including people he could not have even imagined himself liking in the beginning."[10]

"Pray unto the Father with All the Energy of Heart"

Mormon, speaking of charity—"the pure love of Christ"—wrote: "Pray unto the Father with all the energy of heart, that ye may be filled with this love" (Moroni 7:48). Likewise, as we let go of all bitterness and put pettiness behind us, as we pray for and do good to those who have injured us, we must also plead with our Heavenly Father to fill our hearts with the true spirit of forgiveness. President Gordon B. Hinckley prophetically promised that such pleadings will not go unanswered.

"If there be any within the sound of my voice who nurture in their hearts the poisonous brew of enmity toward another, I plead with you to ask the Lord for strength to forgive. . . . It may not be easy, and it may not come quickly. But if you will seek it with sincerity and cultivate it, it *will* come. . . . There will come into your heart a peace otherwise unattainable."[11]

The Savior's injunction, *forgive to be forgiven*, not only provides for the eternal prospect of being cleansed of our own sins, but also offers a very real and much needed promise for the here and now. If we will do our part to forgive and extend mercy and compassion to those who have "stepped on our toes" in some manner, He will fill our hearts with peace. We will come to experience divine love in ways we would not have known otherwise. That is the timeless message of the Savior's simple parable of the unmerciful servant. It is much more than an interesting story. It contains life-changing principles and promises—promises of peace, mercy, and goodwill— promises much needed in this modern world.

Notes

1. Joseph Smith, *Teachings of the Prophet Joseph Smith*, sel. Joseph Fielding Smith [Salt Lake City: Deseret Book, 1976], 256–57.
2. C. S. Lewis, "On Forgiveness," in *The Weight of Glory and Other Addresses*, rev. ed., ed. Walter Hooper (New York: Macmillan, 1949), 121–22, 125; emphasis added.
3. H. Burke Peterson, in Conference Report, October 1983, 83–84.
4. Boyd K. Packer, "Balm of Gilead," *Ensign*, November 1987, 16.
5. Gordon B. Hinckley, in Conference Report, October 1980, 87.
6. Ibid., 86; see also *The Works of Guy de Maupassant* (Roslyn, N.Y.: Black's Reader Service), 34–38.
7. William Dawson, "There Is a Balm in Gilead," *Recreational Songs* (Salt Lake City: The Church of Jesus Christ of Latter-day Saints, 1949), 130.
8. Corrie ten Boom, "I'm Still Learning to Forgive," *Guideposts*, November 1972. "I'm Still Learning to Forgive" by Corrie ten Boom. Reprinted with permission from *Guideposts* magazine. Copyright © 1972 by Guideposts, Carmel, New York 10512.
9. Packer, "Balm of Gilead," 18.
10. C. S. Lewis, *Mere Christianity* (New York: Macmillan, 1952), 108, 116–17.
11. Hinckley, in Conference Report, October 1980, 87.

CHAPTER 5

"HE THAT IS GREATEST AMONG YOU"

What constitutes greatness? What makes something or someone great, as opposed to ordinary, average, or even just plain good? These questions are not easily answered. Perhaps it is because the word *greatness* is not easily defined—especially in a day and age when we so casually attribute greatness to even the most ordinary objects. The words *great* and *greatness* seem to have suffered the same fate as the word *awesome*; and our modern-day slang now turns the majestic into the mundane. "This is the *greatest* hamburger I've ever had!" "You look *great!*" "I just saw the *greatest* movie of all time!" I could list ad nauseum the ways in which I have heard the words *great* and *greatest* used to describe everything and everyone from tomato soup to Mother Theresa. These words have become somewhat synonymous with slang descriptions from past generations. But just because something may be *groovy*, doesn't make it *great*. My wife once said to one of our children, who was oohing and aahing over her new school clothes, "God is awesome. Underwear is not!" In a similar vein, the term *great* applies to the Lord and his true disciples in a much more profound way than we so often use it.

GOODNESS IS MORE DESIRABLE THAN GREATNESS

Even Jesus' disciples, early on in their ministry, had a hard time understanding what constitutes true greatness. On more than one occasion they fought among themselves as to which one of them was the greatest. While the disciples walked with the Master to the village of Capernaum, they had an argument (or what my wife and I prefer to call a "spirited discussion") that Jesus could only partially hear. Upon entering the house, Jesus asked them, "What was it that ye disputed among yourselves by the way?" The Gospel writers, Mark and Matthew, record this unique event.

"But they held their peace: for by the way they had disputed among themselves, who should be the greatest.

"And he sat down, and called the twelve, and saith unto them, If any man desire to be first [the greatest], the same shall be last of all, and servant of all" (Mark 9:34–35).

"At the same time came the disciples unto Jesus, saying, Who is the greatest in the kingdom of heaven?

"And Jesus called a little child unto him, and set him in the midst of them,

"And said, Verily I say unto you, Except ye be converted, and become as little children, ye shall not enter into the kingdom of heaven.

"Whosoever therefore shall humble himself as this little child, the same is greatest in the kingdom of heaven" (Matthew 18:1–4).

It is almost unfathomable that these grown men—dedicated disciples of the Master—could argue over such a seemingly silly thing. Their disputations, however, reflect a lack of spiritual understanding and misguided definitions of greatness. Perhaps they equated prominence or position with greatness. Maybe they believed that the importance of the assignments they received determined their greatness. Did eloquence, intelligence, or persuasiveness in preaching make one of them greater than another whose abilities may have been less? Did the number of miracles performed or converts won determine greatness? Of course not! It is easy for us to read these accounts and scratch our heads in amazement that these disciples could have thought such things. Yet don't we demonstrate similar behavior more than we want to admit? Don't we sometimes equate greatness with remarkable achievements and extraordinary abilities—even fame and wealth? No wonder Jesus called a child to him. Sitting upon his knee was the very example of greatness. The little child had not done mighty works or achieved the pinnacle of success or done anything that would be considered by the world as excellent or eminent. Neither prominence nor prestige nor position made that child a living, flesh and blood symbol of greatness—spiritual greatness, Christlike greatness. What did that little child possess or symbolize that Jesus used to define greatness? Perhaps the answer is so simple that we often "look beyond the mark." True greatness is goodness.

The dictionary defines *great* with terms such as *distinguished, remarkable, mighty, illustrious, important, excellent,* and *renowned.* I would agree that most of those words fit, but none of them really seems to apply to the little child on Jesus' lap—the personification of the Savior's definition of greatness. And while many of the dictionary's definitions for the word *good* are the same as those for *great,* there are some unique exceptions that certainly characterize a little child: *virtuous, honest, kind, pure, moral.*

There are numerous examples of true greatness from the Savior's life and ministry—too many for me, or anyone, to enumerate. Some of these examples, however, seem to literally jump off the pages of the scriptures, profoundly reminding me that I have a ways to go to become like that little child on Jesus' lap— "the greatest in the kingdom of heaven." From these examples come valuable lessons for us about meekness, humility, gratitude, self-sacrifice, quiet service, innocence, kindness, and love—the elements that will make us good, even great.

"Meek and Lowly in Heart"

"In a world too preoccupied with winning through intimidation and seeking to be number one," President Howard W. Hunter observed, "no large crowd of folk is standing in line to buy books that call for mere meekness. But the meek shall inherit the earth, a pretty impressive corporate takeover—and done *without* intimidation."[1] Unfortunately, all too many in the world today think of humility and meekness as undesirable traits, characteristics of weakness, not strength—and certainly not of greatness. Some would define meekness as being weak, lacking ambition or achievement, being subservient or spineless—a sort of doormat for others to walk all over. They would similarly view humility as a lack of self-confidence and assertiveness. The Savior, on the other hand, repeatedly taught that to possess real strength and achieve true greatness and lasting success, one must be as he is—"meek and lowly in heart" (Matthew 11:29; see also Moroni 7:43–44). Jesus certainly could not be characterized as weak and spineless or lacking confidence and competence in his ministry. Nor did he cowardly shrink from difficulties—the "bitter cup" being the most difficult of all—or apologize for or dilute his gospel message and his pointed calls for repentance. "One can be bold and meek at the same time," President Spencer W. Kimball taught. "One can be courageous and humble."[2]

A truly meek person is firm and steadfast but also gentle and kind. Meekness seeks conciliation and understanding, not confrontation or strife. One who emulates the Master's meekness communicates clearly, courageously, and candidly but always with compassion and love—never with malicious intent to hurt and harm. Meekness is mildness of temper—a controlling not only of one's emotions, but also one's expressions. "Meekness, however, is more than self-restraint," Elder Neal A. Maxwell declared, "it is the presentation of self in a posture of kindness and gentleness. It reflects certitude, strength, serenity; it reflects a healthy self-esteem and a genuine self-control."[3]

Meekness, as an attribute of true greatness, also encompasses patience. The "meek and lowly of heart" are long-suffering—not just suffering long but, rather, submitting in faith to both God's *will* and his *timetable*. Meekness means patience with others and self—

looking not just at deficiencies but giving credit for proper direction and righteous desires. Meekness means having *tolerance* for others' differences without having to *tolerate* evil. It is love for the sinner, but hatred of sin. It is kindness, patience, and gentleness in our dealings with others and faithful submission, not coerced or given blindly, to God. True greatness in the eyes of the Lord can never be obtained without meekness.

What of meekness's companion, "lowliness of heart"? What does it mean, and what must we *do* and *be* to become "lowly in heart" as the Savior was and is? If we were to take a poll of one thousand people, asking what they consider to be the ten most important characteristics of Deity, I doubt that "lowliness of heart" would even be mentioned. That trait almost seems incongruous with all that we know concerning God's omniscience and omnipotence. Yet Jesus, the great Jehovah, creator of heavens and earth, the mighty Immanuel—"God with us"—refers to himself as "lowly in heart" (Matthew 11:29). It is interesting that as Jesus made his triumphal entry into Jerusalem just days before his death, he was hailed by throngs as the King of Kings, yet he was seen as lowly because he rode upon a donkey (see Matthew 21:5; also Zechariah 9:9).

We can better understand what is meant by lowliness of heart when we think of the phrase's opposite: highness or haughtiness of heart. We call that pride. President Ezra Taft Benson taught: "Most of us think of pride as self-centeredness, conceit, boastfulness, arrogance, or haughtiness. All of these are elements of the sin, but the heart, or core, is still missing.

"The central feature of pride is enmity—enmity toward God and enmity toward our fellowmen. . . .

"Pride is essentially competitive in nature. We pit our will against God's. When we direct our pride toward God, it is in the spirit of 'my will and not thine be done.' . . .

"The proud cannot accept the authority of God giving

direction to their lives (see Helaman 12:6). They pit their perceptions of truth against God's great knowledge, their abilities versus God's priesthood power, their accomplishments against His mighty works.

"Our enmity toward God takes on many labels, such as rebellion, hard-heartedness, stiff-neckedness, unrepentant, puffed up, easily offended, and sign seekers. The proud wish God would agree with them. They aren't interested in changing their opinions to agree with God's.

"Another major portion of this very prevalent sin of pride is enmity toward our fellowmen. We are tempted daily to elevate ourselves above others and diminish them (see Helaman 6:17; D&C 58:41).

"The proud make every man their adversary by pitting their intellects, opinions, works, wealth, talents, or any other worldly measuring device against others. . . .

" . . . The proud depend upon the world to tell them whether they have value or not. Their self-esteem is determined by where they are judged to be on the ladders of worldly success. They feel worthwhile as individuals if the numbers beneath them in achievement, talent, beauty, or intellect are large enough. Pride is ugly. It says, 'If you succeed, I am a failure.' . . .

" . . . Pride affects all of us at various times and in various degrees. . . .

"Pride is the universal sin, the great vice."[4]

In contrast to the arrogance and stubborn independence of the proud, the Savior taught that true greatness is personified in the simplicity and dependence of a little child who willingly submits to the will of his father (see Matthew 18:4; also Mosiah 3:19). Lowliness of heart is humility, which is, as President Benson taught, the only real "antidote for pride."[5]

Humility is not self-deprecation. "Humility is not the disavowal of our worth," Elder Maxwell wrote, "rather, it is the sober realization of how much we are valued by God."[6] One can be humble and confident, humble and dynamic, humble and successful, humble and powerful. Certainly the Savior was all of that and more. Those who are humble do not have a "woe is me" attitude. The humble man does not put himself down, but neither does he exalt himself. He recognizes that it is Christ who lifts him up. True humility is recognition of the goodness of God in our lives and our realization that all gifts and successes come because of him, not because of us. The truly great man is a humble man who recognizes his mistakes, asks forgiveness, and is willing to change. It is easy to give counsel and correction, but it takes humility to receive it. Humility requires us to be teachable—to seriously take lessons from the Great Schoolmaster and diligently do our "homework" however painful and inconvenient it may be. Humility is doing God's will and seeking his approbation. Humility is giving credit where credit is due—and while many around us deserve much of the credit, the Lord deserves all. Humble evaluation of self—no matter how successful we may become, no matter how talented we may be—brings the stark realization that, as Elder Neal Maxwell so eloquently stated, "any assessment of where we stand in relation to Him tells us that we do not stand at all! We kneel!"[7]

GRATITUDE

Closely akin to meekness and humility is gratitude, another attribute of those who are great in the eyes of God. Gratitude's prideful opposite, however, bespeaks selfishness, self-centeredness, and an unwillingness to recognize (or total oblivion to) the goodness of God and the many kindnesses one continually receives from others. Perhaps nowhere is ingratitude better illustrated than in the story of the ten lepers who were healed by Christ's generous healing power.

"And it came to pass, as [Jesus] went to Jerusalem, that he passed through the midst of Samaria and Galilee.

"And as he entered into a certain village, there met him ten men that were lepers, which stood afar off:

"And they lifted up their voices, and said, Jesus, Master, have mercy on us.

"And when he saw them, he said unto them, Go shew yourselves unto the priests. And it came to pass, that, as they went, they were cleansed.

"And one of them, when he saw that he was healed, turned back, and with a loud voice glorified God,

"And fell down on his face at [Jesus'] feet, giving him thanks: and he was a Samaritan.

"And Jesus answering said, Were there not ten cleansed? but where are the nine?

"There are not found that returned to give glory to God, save this stranger.

"And he said unto him, Arise, go thy way: thy faith hath made thee whole" (Luke 17:11–19).

Each of these ten lepers showed great faith in their pleadings for Jesus to heal them. Yet perhaps even greater than faith was the Samaritan's grateful acknowledgment of his miraculous healing. His gratitude testified of his goodness as well as his faith and, in the end, resulted in a greater blessing. Through faith, ten were cleansed of leprosy—made whole physically. With profound gratitude accentuating his faith, one was made whole spiritually—healed of spiritual sickness and forgiven of sin.

The greatest people I know—those that are truly great in the sight of God—are grateful, always glorifying God for his goodness and blessings and continually expressing appreciation for others. This is graciousness in the truest sense of the word—gratitude and grace go hand in hand. I have seen a woman amidst profound suffering, even on her deathbed, use what little physical strength she had left in her body to express heartfelt appreciation to a caregiver's simplest and most mundane service. That is greatness.

I have seen a child shower his mother with "Thank you, Mommy! Thank you, Mommy!" for a small act of service that would have gone unnoticed by most. That is greatness. Childlike gratitude to Heavenly Father is often expressed in simple yet profound ways. President Harold B. Lee told of hearing the simple prayer of a little boy who prayed, "Dear God, I am glad we can talk to you in these wonderful words, and dear God, I wish there was something I could do for you for all the wonderful things that you have done for us."[8]

I have seen men and women of significant stature in industry and government. I have been privileged to know and work with prominent women and men in high positions of leadership in the Church. Those who are greatest in my estimation consistently and continually express appreciation to those they work with—both above them and below them. I have heard generous expressions of appreciation for all kinds of things—even those things that are just part of doing one's job. Even if the task is required—part of the job description—these good men and women of God express as much sincere gratitude as for those things that go far beyond the call of duty. That is graciousness and gratitude which bespeaks genuine goodness.

LIVING THE GOLDEN RULE

"Therefore all things whatsoever ye would that men should do to you, do ye even so to them," Jesus declared in the Sermon on the Mount, "for this is the law and the prophets" (Matthew 7:12). The Master himself was and is the personification of this "golden rule." We often speak of the Savior's love, but inherent in that perfect love—inherent in his greatness in the eyes of his Father—is also his gentleness, kindness, and consideration of others. Numerous scripture references testify of the loving-kindness of the Lord (see Psalm 51:1; Isaiah 54:8; 63:7; 1 Nephi 19:9; 3 Nephi 22:8–10; D&C 133:52). President David O. McKay taught:

"Kindness is one of the choicest of gems in the coronet of Truth. . . . Christ's short life among men was replete with acts reflecting this divine principle. His kindness won the loving but repentant sinner of Magdala, inspired hope and regeneration of life of the woman sentenced to be stoned to death, and filled gracious mothers' hearts with eternal gratitude as He gently and lovingly blessed their little ones. Thus, just as His strength and perfect faith inspired the hardy fishermen of Galilee, and compelled even rulers of the Jews to seek wisdom and guidance at His feet, so His kindness shed its rays upon those who were weak and tender, guiding them along the pathway to peace and salvation."[9]

The world today seems to say that a person cannot achieve real success—the pinnacle of greatness—without being bossy, assertive, or demanding. Worldly trends have caused us to place larger premiums on these traits than on kindness, courtesy, and patience. We demand results—product is more important than process, success is the "be all and end all"—regardless of what one must do to attain them. These worldly philosophies, or so-called attributes of "greatness," justify treating others unkindly and warrant impatience and curtness in our interactions with others; they become tools for overriding incompetence. Such attitudes and actions are antithetical to the qualities of goodness and greatness that Jesus taught his disciples. Rudeness, impatience, and a lack of concern for the feelings of others might be characteristic of the natural man, but are never attributes of the man or woman of Christ.

When I observe acts of unkindness, insensitive or inconsiderate comments, or any form of treatment of others that is antithetical to Christ's goodness and kindness, I have begun taking inventory of my own treatment of others:

- Do I treat my students or office help with less deference, patience, and kindness than I would my boss or a General Authority?

- Do I feel justified in being unkind or insensitive to those "under me" but would never act that way to those "over me"?
- Do I treat members of my own family with less kindness and courtesy than I treat mere acquaintances or even strangers?

"Courtesy is not unusual conduct to be reserved for a special circle of friends or circumstances," Elder Marvin J. Ashton wrote. "It is not a veneer to be put on for special social occasions or people. It is a way of life of tremendous significance, whether it be in the home, in the office, or on the highway. . . . We cannot justify or condone discourtesy regardless of friendship or situation."[10]

Truly great people—Christlike people who emulate his goodness—will live the Golden Rule and treat all God's children with kindness and courtesy. "The measure of a man is not necessarily his title or position," Elder Victor L. Brown testified, *but rather how he treats others.*"[11] More than we often suspect, the attributes of "godly greatness"—kindness, patience, consideration, and just being nice—touch the most lives and yield unsung and unseen dividends. As an anonymous writer once penned:

> *I have wept in the night*
> *For the shortness of sight*
> *That to somebody's need made me blind;*
> *But I never have yet*
> *Felt a tinge of regret*
> *For being a little too kind.*

THE WIDOW'S MITE

At the Last Supper, Jesus' disciples once again contended among themselves over "which of them should be accounted the greatest" (Luke 22:24). Jesus rebuked them and reminded them that greatness to God is much different—higher and more significant—from the world's view of greatness. Worldly and "natural" men strive among themselves over such things as position, social status, and even where one sits at a state dinner. "But ye shall not be so," Jesus said. "He that is greatest among you, let him be as the younger; and he that is chief, as he that doth serve. For whether is greater, he that sitteth at meat, or he that serveth? is not he that sitteth at meat? but I am among you as he that serveth" (Luke 22:26–27). In his tender rebuke, the Master—the greatest of all—taught his disciples that true greatness comes not from where you sit or who you sit by, but by how you serve.

At this significant paschal feast—the last Passover of the Savior's earthly ministry—where Jesus would profoundly and clearly teach about his impending atoning sacrifice, he viewed himself not as the guest of honor but as the servant of all. To illustrate the inextricable link between greatness and service, Jesus laid aside his robe and "took a towel and girded himself" and washed the feet of his disciples. It was customary that a lowly servant (in some settings a slave) be clothed in a towel-like cloak and perform the most menial of courtesies—washing the feet of the guests. Can you imagine what the disciples must have thought and felt as they saw the greatest man they had ever known—the very Son of God—descend to the level of a common servant or slave? That was his point precisely! "He that is greatest among you shall be your servant," Jesus declared (Matthew 23:11). A truly great person does not exalt himself, but serves all on all levels. To God, there is no such thing as unimportant service. "Low profile" service is as significant, if not more so, than "high profile" service. In fact, as Jesus taught and exemplified, sometimes the simple, quiet, and unheralded acts of service are the greatest acts of true discipleship.

On one occasion, as Jesus and his disciples were on the Temple Mount near the treasury, they observed people making their monetary contributions. Some of the rich were making quite a show of their wealth as they cast several coins into the treasury. One person, however, attracted the Master's attention and elicited an important teaching moment.

"And there came a certain poor widow, and she threw in two mites, which make a farthing.

"And he called unto him his disciples, and saith unto them, Verily I say unto you, That this poor widow hath cast more in, than all they which have cast into the treasury:

"For all they did cast in of their abundance; but she of her want did cast in all that she had, even all her living" (Mark 12:42–44).

In the eyes of the Lord, this poor widow made a more significant contribution than all of the rich men combined. Greatness was not then, nor is it now, determined by the amount sacrificed *but by the willingness to sacrifice*. This principle applies to actions and attitudes as well. Today there are truly great people who, like the widow and her mites, make contributions of time and energy in service to others. Most often this service takes place behind the scenes—hidden from the view of most and unheralded by publicity. Those who serve this way do so in many forms. They may be caring for an aged parent—emptying bedpans, massaging arthritic limbs, or brushing teeth. They may be the parents of a handicapped child, who day after day attend to the most simple and mundane of needs. Their service isn't pretty and it isn't easy. Among these is the single parent who reads to a child or helps him with homework, even amidst overwhelming fatigue after a long day at work. These people are the moms and dads who love their children with all their hearts, teach them the gospel, exemplify righteousness in their lives, and never stop praying for the welfare of their families. They include the single person who desperately desires a loving marriage but does not wallow in self-pity; rather, she faithfully serves and loves and strengthens those around her. You don't see these people on the ten o'clock news. Their faces are not on the covers of today's popular magazines. They do not receive the applause and accolades of the world. Yet they truly are the great ones because of their willingness to sacrifice part of themselves, to render service no matter how difficult, and to attend to duty no matter how small. President Joseph F. Smith taught:

"To do well those things which God ordained to be the common lot of all man-kind, is the truest greatness. To be a successful father or a successful mother is greater than to be a successful general or a successful statesman. . . .

"We should never be discouraged in those daily tasks which God has ordained to the common lot of man. Each day's labor should be undertaken in a joyous spirit and with the thought and conviction that our happiness and eternal welfare depend upon doing well that which we ought to do, that which God has made it our duty to do."[12]

Service, sacrifice, and attention to duty don't always come in the form of callings or service projects. In fact, the kind of service that Jesus told his disciples was characteristic of "he that is greatest among you" doesn't require a sign-up sheet or an assignment from a leader. It simply involves perceiving a need and doing something, however simple or mundane, that lifts a burden, comforts another, or blesses a life. It is doing and giving our best, even if that isn't a lot.

A few years ago I was bedridden with a seriously herniated disc in my spine. It was too painful to get out of bed and get dressed. My family took good care of me and there wasn't any glaring need at home. If my home teachers had called and asked if there was anything they could do, I would have appreciated their call but probably would have told them there was nothing they could do. My neighbor, however, didn't call to ask. He just came over and mowed my lawn and didn't say anything about it. He wasn't my home teacher or a quorum or ward leader. He hadn't been assigned or even volunteered for "a project." He just did it, because that is the kind of person he is. He may not have thought that his service was very significant. I am convinced, however, that when the real story of his life is told among the heavenly hosts, his acts of simple service will carry greater worth than most of the accomplishments, positions, possessions, and social status of others who are viewed as great. More than just the act of mowing my lawn, my neighbor's life of quiet, unheralded service characterizes what Jesus taught concerning true greatness—the server is greater than he who merely dines. As some anonymous person once observed: "True greatness and lasting happiness come to those who have windows in their lives, not mirrors."

"HE MUST INCREASE, BUT I MUST DECREASE"

We are familiar with Jesus' own actions used to teach us what greatness means in the eyes of God: bringing a little child to his knee, donning the servant-towel to wash the feet of his disciples. In addition, Jesus used another real-life person as an example of greatness. "Verily I say unto you, Among them that are born of women," the Savior declared, "there hath not risen a greater than John the Baptist" (Matthew 11:11). What was it about this man— this "wild" man from the desert clothed in camel hair, eating locusts and wild honey, who cried repentance unto the people (Matthew 3:1–11)—that made him so great in the eyes of Christ? What traits of godly greatness did he possess? What do we learn from his life that we can emulate in our own?

While the unique aspect of John's ministry—his role as forerunner of the Messiah—is not something we have been called to do, there is an element of his greatness that can easily be incorporated into our own lives. It is found in a statement he made to his followers. These disciples had heard the powerful teachings of Jesus of Nazareth and had witnessed Jesus' mighty works. Torn between what they had seen and heard and their devotion to John, they asked the Baptist if Jesus was the Messiah they should follow. John's answer bespeaks his greatness and his recognition that, although his foreordained ministry was important—like no other in history—there was still One greater, even the Greatest of All.

"Ye yourselves bear me witness, that I said, I am not the Christ, but that I am sent before him.

"He that hath the bride is the bridegroom: but the friend of the bridegroom, which standeth and heareth him, rejoiceth greatly because of the bridegroom's voice: this my joy therefore is fulfilled.

"*He must increase, but I must decrease*" (John 3:28–30; emphasis added).

John's mission was to prepare the way for the Messiah. His teachings were to prepare the hearts of his listeners for the greater message of Christ. Therefore, he gladly directed his disciples to the Master and testified of His divinity. There was no competing for popularity or for disciples. He fully understood that his role was to lead souls to Christ, not to stand in their way or distract them from the Lord's saving power.

Each of us, like John, should lead souls to Christ. We should come to clearly understand that all we do and say—the very reason why we serve—is not to bring glory to ourselves, but to help others come unto Christ. We can feed and nurture, teach and lead, strengthen and serve, but only the Savior can change hearts, bring forgiveness, spiritually transform lives, and ultimately save us. One who is great in the sight of God does not seek to bring disciples to himself. We can lead the sheep and lambs to the Good Shepherd—but they are his flock, not ours! A great person recognizes that he need not be in the limelight, because there is indeed only one Light that matters—the Light of the World.

There is another aspect of John's forerunner greatness that, I believe, has particular meaning to us today. John performed spiritually significant service, but he wasn't the "star of the show." That role rightfully and solely belonged to Jesus. You don't have to be the star to achieve greatness. In fact, most often, godly greatness is manifest in those who act in "supporting roles"—coaching and coaxing the "lead actors," building and decorating the set, shining the lights in just the right way so that others will look their best.

I came to see this principle in operation most dramatically when I served as a bishop. The bishop has the "starring role" for the ward, but he can't remember his lines without the help of others. One Sunday, as I prepared to conduct sacrament meeting, I received a frantic message from a ward member that the ward organist was sick. She would not be there, and unfortunately no one else knew the hymns we were to sing. Then I received another frantic message—there was no bread for the sacrament. I guess it could have been worse—the speakers could have not come, the power could have suddenly blacked out, the chorister could have passed out, and my zipper could have been down! There came to me a stark realization at that moment—and I have appreciated it many times since—that supportive roles and behind-the-scenes service is very often that which matters most. It is, in fact, that which makes all the difference.

How grateful I am for my own wife, who does not seek the limelight but who supports me in my righteous endeavors, encourages me when I'm discouraged, suggests needed improvements for my life, loves me no matter what, and sometimes picks up the pieces. Her support is far greater than any of my own accomplishments. She is not the only one in my life who has been the real hero. She is like countless others—men and women, young and old—whose contributions may not be visible to the masses, but are invaluable nonetheless. All of us are products of the behind-the-scenes love and labor of the countless support staff in our lives. Each of us knows people who are not in the limelight, whose supportive work is rarely noticed yet makes all the difference to the success of programs and people. These individuals genuinely rejoice in the success, accomplishments, and glory that the star of the show gets as a result. Often it requires greater goodness and humility to serve and support in such a way that will bring honor and recognition to another, and perhaps no recognition to the actual doer. Who is greater—the prophet, or his wife that supports and strengthens him and faithfully shares him with the Church? Who is greater—the Gospel Doctrine teacher who can expound the scriptures and clarify the mysteries of the kingdom, or the Primary chorister who helps children praise God in song? Who is greater and deserves the greatest recognition—the Eagle Scout, or his mother? What is greater—the majestic eagle in flight, or the wind beneath his wings? To the godly great there is willingness to serve and support without public recognition or universal notice, because of the conviction that One knows and takes note—and that One is all that really matters.

Becoming as a Little Child

Each of the various attributes that this chapter has addressed—meekness, humility, gratitude, kindness, service—are among those qualities of greatness that Jesus urged his disciples to acquire. Still, these traits by themselves, either separately or together, do not fully qualify one for the greatness of which Jesus spoke—greatness "in the kingdom of heaven."

"And Jesus called a little child unto him, and set him in the midst of them,

"And said, Verily I say unto you, Except ye be converted, and become as little children, ye shall not enter into the kingdom of heaven.

"Whosoever therefore shall humble himself as this little child, the same is greatest in the kingdom of heaven" (Matthew 18:1–4). What is it that Jesus teaches us with his admonition to become as little children? We often look at that phrase and think to ourselves: *Little children are sweet and innocent, submissive and gentle.* Are those things that Jesus meant for us to become? Yes. But if you think about it carefully, there must be more to becoming like a little child than simply behaving in those ways. Can little children be not-so-gentle, even mean? Yes. Can they be strongly independent and stubborn (anything but submissive), even disobedient? Of course. Are all little children equally humble and teachable? If only that were true! What, then, did Jesus mean? How does becoming like a little child qualify one as "the greatest in the kingdom of heaven"? The answer is found in the phrase, "except ye be converted." Converted to what? To Christ, of course. Meekness, humility, gentleness, gratitude, and service are all admirable traits and will do much to refine an individual. They do not, however, bring someone to conversion and make him like a little child. They may be means to that end, but they are not *the* end.

Looking carefully at the Beatitudes—which call upon us to be meek, humble, submissive, and so on—teaches us something more about becoming as a little child. The traits mentioned in those famous passages are desirable qualities and will do much to bless the individual and society. Yet something is missing from the version we read in the New Testament. The poor in spirit, just because they are humble, are not guaranteed exaltation in the kingdom of heaven. The meek, just because they are meek, do not automatically inherit the earth—either in this life or the next. In the Book of Mormon account, however, the resurrected Christ attaches this phrase to each of these important traits: "who come unto me" (3 Nephi 12:3, 19–20). Clearly, greatness in the kingdom of heaven—"worlds without end"—can never be obtained by our own merits or goodness. We become like a little child when we come unto Christ, become converted to his gospel, and are cleansed by his atonement. It takes childlike humility and submission to do this. As King Benjamin taught his own people:

"For the natural man is an enemy to God, and has been from the fall of Adam, and will be, forever and ever, unless he yields to the enticings of the Holy Spirit, and putteth off the natural man and becometh a saint *through the atonement of Christ the Lord, and becometh as a child,* submissive, meek, humble, patient, full of love, willing to submit to all things which the Lord seeth fit to inflict upon him, even as a child doth submit to his father" (Mosiah 3:19; emphasis added).

Becoming as a child constitutes true greatness in the eyes of the Lord. To sit down with the noble and great ones in the kingdom of God will require inward goodness, not outward achievement. The great ones there will possess the attributes of humility and meekness, kindness and gentleness. They will personify patience and gratitude, sacrifice and service. Their lives will have been lives of love. Most of all, however, the truly great will have become as blameless as little children. Such innocence and purity is obtained, as King Benjamin testified, "only through repentance and faith on the name of the Lord God Omnipotent" (Mosiah 3:21). Becoming as a little child through the atonement of Christ brings not only purity resulting from a remission of sins, but much more. "And the remission of sins," declared Mormon, "bringeth meekness, and lowliness of heart; and because of meekness and lowliness of heart cometh the visitation of the Holy Ghost, which Comforter filleth with hope and perfect love, which love endureth by diligence unto prayer, until the end shall come, when all the saints shall dwell with God" (Moroni 8:26). That is true greatness! It is the greatness of Christ! And that is what we seek at his hands. His greatness will make me great in God's sight and I will be able to sit down in the Father's kingdom with all the great ones of the ages, *if I will come unto him*. His goodness and mercy combined with my faith in him and my own childlike submission to his gospel will make me good. That is true greatness!

Notes

1. Howard W. Hunter, *The Teachings of Howard W. Hunter,* ed. Clyde J. Williams (Salt Lake City: Bookcraft, 1997), 266.

2. Spencer W. Kimball, *Humility* (BYU Devotional Address, 16 January 1963), Provo, Utah: Brigham Young University Press, 1963, 2.

3. Neal A. Maxwell, "Meekly Drenched in Destiny," *Brigham Young University 1982–83 Fireside and Devotional Speeches* (Provo, Utah: Brigham Young University, 1983), 2.
4. Ezra Taft Benson, in Conference Report, April 1989, 3–6.
5. Ibid., 6.
6. Neal A. Maxwell, *All These Things Shall Give Thee Experience* (Salt Lake City: Deseret Book, 1979), 127.
7. Neal A. Maxwell, in Conference Report, October 1981, 9.
8. As cited in *The Teachings of Harold B. Lee*, ed. Clyde J. Williams (Salt Lake City: Bookcraft, 1996), 194.
9. David O. McKay, *Pathways to Happiness*, comp. Llewelyn R. McKay (Salt Lake City: Bookcraft, 1957), 149.
10. Marvin J. Ashton, *What Is Your Destination?* (Salt Lake City: Deseret Book, 1978), 110.
11. Victor L. Brown, in Conference Report, October 1989, 96; emphasis added.
12. Joseph F. Smith, *Gospel Doctrine*, 5th ed. (Salt Lake City: Deseret Book, 1939), 285.

CHAPTER 6

"YE CANNOT SERVE GOD AND MAMMON"

When I was a young boy of about six or seven, our family took the traditional pilgrimage to Disneyland in California. The drive from southeastern Idaho seemed like it would never end as I anxiously fantasized about the fun and excitement awaiting me in the Magic Kingdom. If the journey seemed endless to me, it must have been worse for my parents as I repeatedly asked, "How much further?" or "When will we be there?" They probably heard those questions a million times. Because they were good parents, they tried to occupy my time and attention with distractions such as treats and games. Finally, after exhausting the treat bag and playing every travel game then known to man, my father suggested a new game. "Brent," he asked, pointing way out in front of us, "see that puddle in the middle of the road? Start counting and see how many seconds it takes until we splash through it."

I gazed intently at the shiny puddle of water that crossed the road. "One thousand one, one thousand two, one thousand three," I counted aloud. After counting to nearly a hundred—with my Dad chuckling in the front seat—I exclaimed, "Wait a second! We never splash through the puddle. What's going on?" I was very serious and quite troubled by what I didn't understand. The rest of the family had a good laugh at my expense. "It's a mirage," my older brother declared amidst the laughter in the car. I had never heard the word before and I didn't have any idea what it meant. "What's a mirage?" I queried. The explanation given me didn't make much

97

sense to my little-boy mind, but at the least I understood that a mirage wasn't what it appeared to be; and no matter how hard and fast I chased after it, I would never catch it.

In the years since my dad pulled that "trick" on me I have used it a time or two with my own children. They all now know what a mirage is. And many years later, I chuckle when I think about how my family was entertained at my expense. There is a serious message, however, attached to this funny family experience. Many times since my first encounter with the elusive mirage I have thought about how we, as mere mortals, often chase after mirages—sometimes even knowing full well that they are illusions. The practical joke my father played on me was harmless; though it did cause me some degree of embarrassment. Unfortunately, the mirages that many people chase today are not so harmless; they are, in reality, a dangerous threat to both spiritual and temporal well-being. One mirage to which I refer is the "mirage of materialism."

The Savior often warned his disciples of the seductiveness of worldly wealth and the spiritual distraction that can result when one chases after it. "Lay not up for yourselves treasures upon earth, where moth and rust doth corrupt, and where thieves break through and steal," Jesus taught in the Sermon on the Mount. "But lay up for yourselves treasures in heaven, where neither moth nor rust doth corrupt, and where thieves do not break through nor steal: *For where your treasure is, there will your heart be also*" (Matthew 6:19–21; emphasis added).

On another occasion, a man (perhaps a Pharisee seeking to trap Jesus in his words) sought mediation from the Master concerning a family financial dispute. The man felt that he was being deprived by his brother of his birthright inheritance, as outlined in the law of Moses. Jesus took the opportunity to warn against covetousness and to teach the true meaning of wealth. "Take heed, and beware of covetousness," the Son of God declared, "for a man's life consisteth not in the abundance of the things which he possesseth" (Luke 12:15).

None of us is immune to the "mirage of materialism" and the spiritual hazards accompanying it—particularly in a society that has been abundantly blessed with unparalleled affluence and economic progress. Perhaps Jesus' words and warnings are more relevant to us today than they were two millennia ago. In the nineteenth century, President Brigham Young declared: "I am more afraid of covetousness [and materialism] in our Elders, than I am of the hordes of hell."[1] From the outset of the Restoration to our very own day, prophets and apostles have warned concerning the spiritual dangers of materialism—what President Ezra Taft Benson called "one of the real plagues of our generation."[2] President Harold B. Lee also taught that today's ease and prosperity may be as much a curse as a blessing. This challenge—what he characterized as the "test of gold"—may in fact be "the most severe test of any age."

"During the early days of the Church we passed through a period of slander and misrepresentation, and we came through. It drove us together because of enemies from the outside. And we survived it. We passed through a period of mobbing and driving, when lives were taken and blood was shed, and somehow the place of the martyr gave us strength. We passed through poverty, and we gained strength from the test of it. Then we passed through an age of what we might call apostasy, or betrayal from the inside—one of the severest tests through which we have passed. . . .

"But today we are being tested and tried by another kind of test that I might call the 'test of gold'—the test of plenty, affluence, ease—more than perhaps the youth of any generation have passed through, at least in this church. . . .

"May the Latter-day Saint youth, youth the noble birthright, whose parents have passed through the rigors of trial and testing, consider now the trials through which they are passing today—ease and luxury and perhaps too easy ways to learning and education. *Theirs may be the most severe test of any age.* God grant that they will not fail, that they will develop the faith that can keep them true when they are in the darkness and humble when they are in the spotlight."[3]

What lessons must we learn and heed from the teachings of the Savior that can help us pass this "most severe test of any age"? Three specific themes are of particular interest and importance to me (and perhaps to all of us) and serve as a clear warning. They are (1) the eternal insignificance of the things of the world, (2) the spiritual dangers of priority distraction and divided loyalties, and (3) the responsibilities accompanying economic prosperity.

"That Which Cannot Satisfy"

Neither Jesus nor prophets before or after him have universally condemned wealth or the positive things that can result from it. They have not advocated misery and malnutrition or exalted poverty as a saving virtue. What seems to be clearly taught is the proper perspective concerning wealth—its limitations and potential pitfalls. Money doesn't seem to be the issue. The fundamental issue seems to be the need for proper priorities based on an eternal perspective. The Lord has declared that the riches and resources of the world are to be used for the blessing of God's children (see Jacob 2:19; Alma 1:29; D&C 38:17–18, 39). Disciples of Christ cannot be totally oblivious to the need for material means. The "riches of the earth" also have a divine purpose. The Savior taught his disciples to recognize that even though the *riches of the earth* fill an important need for mankind, they are not as vital as the *riches of eternity.* The former will ultimately perish, the latter will not. President Ezra Taft Benson used an interesting metaphor to highlight this principle. "Material treasures of earth are merely to provide us, as it were, room and board while we are here at school."[4] Room and board are important commodities at college, but they do not provide the desired and needed education—no matter how nice the apartment or how delicious the food. Similarly, material means may help to make life passable—even comfortable, and convenient—yet they do not in any way provide the essential spiritual passport to God's presence.

The Savior used a simple allegory, known as the parable of the rich fool, to illustrate this concept:

"The ground of a certain rich man brought forth plentifully:

"And he thought within himself, saying, What shall I do, because I have no room where to bestow my fruits?

"And he said, This will I do: I will pull down my barns, and build greater; and there will I bestow all my fruits and my goods.

"And I will say to my soul, Soul, thou hast much goods laid up for many years; take thine ease, eat, drink, and be merry.

"But God said unto him, Thou fool, this night thy soul shall be required of thee: then whose shall those things be, which thou hast provided?

"So is he that layeth up treasure for himself, and is not rich toward God" (Luke 12:16–21).

The rich fool's many barns filled with "much goods" did nothing to pave the way for a pleasant passage for his soul into heaven. He stood naked before his maker, taking only those things with him that had spiritual worth. His nice house, his prosperous business, his attractive attire, and his temporal toys were all left behind in the physical world. They possessed no value in the spiritual realm, nor bespoke in any way the state of his soul. As the Savior declared: "A man's life [or we could say a man's soul] consisteth not in the abundance of the things which he possesseth" (Luke 12:15), and further, "The life is more than meat, and the body is more than raiment" (Luke 12:23). Perhaps President Spencer W. Kimball said it best when he asked, "What honor is there in being the richest man in the cemetery?"[5]

Seeking for and acquiring earthly riches is somewhat like

building a sandcastle on the seashore. We may go to a lot of effort and even construct a remarkably complex and detailed structure— one that is both admired and envied. Eventually, however, when high tide inevitably comes (or morning storm squalls), the elaborate castle will once again become a pile of sand. Within a very short time, in fact, it won't even be a pile anymore, but merely an indistinguishable part of the seashore. Like mirages, sandcastles look grand and impressive for a short time; but in the end, they are not really what they appear to be and aren't ever as great as we thought. No wonder Jesus repeatedly reminded us that wealth and the things of the world are, at best, of limited temporary worth, and most often illusionary and elusive. "We ought to care no more for the silver and the gold, and the property that is so much sought for by the wicked world," President Brigham Young declared, "than for the soil or the gravel upon which we tread."[6]

"Do not spend money for that which is of no worth, nor your labor for that which cannot satisfy," the prophet Isaiah declared (2 Nephi 9:51). We all have to buy food to eat, clothes to wear, and shelter in which to live. Therefore, it is not likely that Isaiah is saying we shouldn't spend money or labor for these things. I do believe, however, that he is reminding us that, like mirages and sandcastles, the things of the world will not and cannot bring us lasting happiness, personal peace, or spiritual satisfaction.

Perhaps that is what Samuel the Lamanite really meant when he prophesied that the Nephites would one day cry "all things [all our earthly possessions] are become slippery, and we cannot hold them" (Helaman 13:36). I don't think their possessions literally became too slick to hold. And I'm not sure they magically or mystically disappeared. The "slipperiness" of the Nephite riches, at least in my estimation, could have been that they had no staying power—no eternal value, no power to produce peace or happiness in this life or a fullness of joy in the next. Hence, the Nephites, like the rich fool, could not hold on to their wealth when it really mattered. In fact, as we see throughout the holy scriptures, materialism almost always yields pride, and pride always disrupts personal peace rather than procuring it. This can easily become a vicious cycle in which we seek greater and greater gratification with things but in reality find less and less satisfaction. This chasing the mirage of materialism leaves us wanting more—no matter how much we obtain. As President Brigham Young taught: "Men and women who are trying to make themselves happy in the possession of wealth or power will miss it, for nothing short of the Gospel of the Son of God can make the inhabitants of the earth happy, and prepare them to enjoy heaven here and hereafter."[7]

My wife and I learned a valuable lesson about this several years ago when we had the opportunity to build a new home. During the months of planning and building, an interesting phenomenon occurred. Even though we were blessed to have a nice home with more comforts than we had ever had before, we began looking for ways to acquire more. We had to have new furniture for the upstairs family room so that we could put the old furniture downstairs (perish the thought that a room might be void of furniture!). But the old entertainment center, a large piece of furniture that held our stereo and TV equipment, didn't go well with the new furniture, so of course, we had to have a new entertainment center. But our old "dark ages" record player didn't look good in the new entertainment center. So we needed a new compact disc player with all the latest technological "bells and whistles." When we obtained the new CD player, of course, we had to replace our outdated record collection by buying a whole new library of expensive CDs. It all seemed so logical and justifiable (at least at the time I was in the electronics store). We soon found that after every new purchase we were faced with numerous other attractive things that appeared necessary and justifiable. It was a never-ending cycle; the more we got, the more we wanted (even justifying it by saying we needed it). I came to understand very clearly that the terms "basic necessities" and "just wants" are relative. What is perceived as a "basic necessity" to my teenage daughter (who often pleads with us saying, "I *have to* have this!"), for example, I might consider an unnecessary and excessive luxury. Our situation with the new house, brought out a lot of "just wants" in me.

Instead of feeling happy with our new home and grateful for the blessings of the Lord in our lives and content with what we had (which was more than we ever thought we would have), we instead felt frustrated at not being able to have all we wanted. Instead of experiencing fulfillment and gratitude, we found ourselves fretting about draperies and landscaping, and worrying about whether we would be able to afford what we wanted and how we were going to pay for the things we had purchased.

This experience has caused me to examine the Master's teachings concerning wealth and possessions—particularly the parable of the rich fool—in a new light. Materialism truly is a mirage. I learned—a painful, but necessary tutorial—that as Jesus declared nearly two millennia ago, true "abundance of life" isn't determined by what one possesses; it is determined by what one *is* and what one *loves*. When "all we've ever wanted" is grounded in the temporal trappings of this world, it is never enough—and can never satisfy the soul! As Elder Neal A. Maxwell once observed, "Large bank accounts [cannot] fill the empty vault of the soul."[8]

THE SPIRITUAL DANGERS OF DIVIDED LOYALTIES

As important as it was to teach his disciples the doctrine of the relative insignificance of riches in the eternal scheme of things, the Savior had another, even more important, objective in his messages regarding materialism. He was raising a warning voice concerning the spiritual consequences that inevitably result from the distraction and diversion of divided loyalties. "Ye cannot serve God and mammon" (Matthew 6:24), Jesus declared in the Sermon on the Mount. What did he mean by that? *Mammon* is the

Aramaic (the native language of the Savior) word for "property" and is sometimes translated as "riches." Was Jesus saying a person cannot faithfully serve God and still work for a living, provide for his family, or even possess some of the comforts and conveniences that material means can provide? Absolutely not! He wasn't saying, "You cannot serve God and *have* money or property." The key seems to be in the word *serve*. Earlier in the same verse, the Master states, "No man can *serve* two masters: for either he will *hate* the one, and *love* the other; or else he will *hold* to the one, and *despise* the other" (emphasis added). These are strong words! The Savior's words in an earlier verse shed perhaps the most light on his warning: "For where your treasure is, there will your heart be also" (Matthew 6:21).

The heart is often used to symbolize love; but this type of love is more than mere affection. It is total devotion, allegiance, and commitment. With this in mind, perhaps we can paraphrase what Jesus said: "You give your total devotion—whole heart, soul, and complete commitment—to that which is most important to you." This brings us to the heart of the matter. The Savior seems to be asking you and me: "Do you love me with all your soul—more than all the things of the world? Are you more attached to the riches of the earth than devoted to the service and commitment required to receive the riches of eternity? Are your attention and efforts more focused on making money and acquiring things than in serving me and your fellowmen?" It may be easier to *give* the right answer to these questions than to truly *live* the right answer.

One episode in the Lord's life clearly illustrates this principle. A rich young ruler approached the Savior and on bended knee humbly asked, "Good Master, what shall I do that I may inherit eternal life?" (Mark 10:17). Jesus reminded him of the need to keep the commandments of God: "Do not commit adultery, Do not kill, Do not steal, Do not bear false witness, Defraud not, Honor thy father and mother" (Mark 10:19). The wealthy young man reported that he had devoutly kept the commandments all his life.

"Then Jesus beholding him loved him, and said unto him, One thing thou lackest: go thy way, sell whatsoever thou hast, and give to the poor, and thou shalt have treasure in heaven: and come, take up the cross, and follow me.

"And he was sad at that saying, and went away grieved: for he had great possessions" (Mark 10:21–22).

That which the young ruler lacked was total devotion to God. He said he loved God, but obviously not as much as he loved mammon—his riches and property. He failed the test not because he was rich, neither because he was wicked, but because he could not or would not totally devote himself to the riches of eternity and let go of the riches of the world. The rich young ruler did not have a money problem—he had a heart problem. His heart—his allegiance, his devotion, his priorities—prevented him from turning his back on the great and spacious building and clinging to the iron rod with both hands.

The Joseph Smith Translation of this account provides us an interesting insight into Jesus' reaction to the rich young ruler. It clarifies what the real problem was for the young ruler then and what the potential danger is for us today.

"And Jesus looked round about, and said unto his disciples, How hardly shall they that have riches enter into the kingdom of my Father!

"And the disciples were astonished at his words. But Jesus spake again and said unto them, Children, how hard is it for them *who trust in riches* to enter into the kingdom of God!

"It is easier for a camel to go through the eye of a needle, than for a rich man to enter into the kingdom of God.

"And they were astonished out of measure, saying among themselves, Who then can be saved?

"And Jesus, looking upon them, said, With men *that trust in riches*, it is impossible; but not impossible with men *who trust in God and leave all for my sake*, for with such all these things are possible" (JST Mark 10:22–26; emphasis added).

None of us would say that we put more trust, devotion, and allegiance in the "things of the world" than in God. Neither would have the rich young ruler. How then did it happen? How did his treasure become his god? The answer is simple—little by little. Sometimes the dangerous divided loyalties start out with seemingly simple, subtle choices that seem innocent and justifiable. Yet over time we become distracted from the things of God and diverted into paths and pursuits that lead us away from what the apostle Paul called, "the unsearchable riches of Christ" (Ephesians 3:8). Even a little distraction can yield terrible consequences. "We get sidetracked by submitting to temptations that divert us past the bounds of safety," Elder Joseph B. Wirthlin taught. "Satan knows our weaknesses. He puts attractive snares on our paths at just those moments when we are most vulnerable. His intent is to lead us from the way that returns us to our Heavenly Father. Sin may result from activities that begin innocently or that are perfectly legitimate in moderation, but in excess, they can cause us to veer from the straight and narrow path to our destruction. . . .

" . . . [One] temptation to detour us is placing improper emphasis on the obtaining of material possessions. For example, we may build a beautiful, spacious home that is far larger than we need. We may spend far too much to decorate, furnish, and landscape it. And even if we are blessed enough to afford such luxury, we may be misdirecting resources that could be better used to build the kingdom of God or to feed and clothe our needy brothers and sisters."⁹

Interestingly, the Savior alluded to this principle in the parable of the sower (sometimes called the parable of the four kinds of soil). In this parable, Jesus explained that the good seed—the word of God—sometimes does not take root in a person's life and is thus unable to "bring fruit to perfection" because it has been "choked with cares and riches and pleasures of this life" (see Luke 8:11–15). The word *choked* is enlightening because it connotes a slow process of suffocation, blocking the spiritual airways with temporal barriers that prevent the "breath of life"—the life-saving and life-sustaining things of God—from entering into our very souls. If we look at this in another way, we understand that a weed chokes a good plant by robbing it of the needed nutrients and overgrowing it, leaving no room for the good plant to adequately grow. This diversion may not seem suffocating at first, but the resultant consequences can be spiritually deadly.

The plague of materialism is not just a rich man's disease, and Jesus' warnings were not directed solely to the wealthy. Paul taught that money is not the "root of all evil"; rather, it is the love of money (see 1 Timothy 6:10). Both rich and poor (and everyone in between) can be guilty of chasing after the materialism mirage. The rich don't have a corner on possessing insatiable appetites for the things that money can buy. The poor can likewise be consumed with greediness, covetousness, and envy. You don't have to be rich to have the spiritual things of God "choked out" because of an unrighteous desire for and devotion to the things of the world. In this dispensation, the Lord warned both the rich and poor against this:

"Wo unto you rich men, that will not give your substance to the poor, for your riches will canker your souls; and this shall be your lamentation in the day of visitation, and of judgment, and of indignation: The harvest is past, the summer is ended, and my soul is not saved!

"Wo unto you poor men, whose hearts are not broken, whose spirits are not contrite, and whose bellies are not satisfied, and whose hands are not stayed from laying hold upon other men's goods, whose eyes are full of greediness, and who will not labor with your own hands!" (D&C 56:16–17).

In this world it is easy to become distracted and diverted from the things that have eternal significance; but this is especially true in times of material prosperity. If we spend our time and energies chasing after the "mirage of materialism," we may soon become spiritually malnourished, although we have plenty to eat and think we are healthy and strong. Because we are serving the wrong master, we may not even know we are missing any nourishment. We may think our lives are full when, in reality, we are deficient of the very things that would give us an abundant life.

This type of spiritual deprivation ultimately leads, if unchecked, to letting go of the iron rod and becoming lost in the "mists of darkness." Thus, distraction and diversion may start out subtly, but end in much greater temptations and transgressions. You can't serve two masters, nor can you give your all to both. Only one leads to eternal wealth. Ultimately, the master—the treasure—you love the most will win out and take you with it. "I would rather not own one farthing," President Brigham Young once observed, "and beg my bread from door to door, than to neglect my duty and lose the Spirit of Almighty God."[10] On another occasion he made this observation concerning members of the Church who seek to serve both God and mammon:

"The Latter-day Saints who turn their attention to money-making soon become cold in their feelings toward the ordinances of the house of God. They neglect their prayers, become unwilling to pay any donations; the law of tithing gets to be too great a task for them; and they finally forsake their God, and the providences of heaven seem to be shut from them—all in consequence of this lust after the things of this world, which will certainly perish in handling, and in their use they will fade away and go from us."[11]

I have often wondered who was more sad, the rich young ruler who could not let go of his worldly possessions to follow the Lord, or the Son of God who lost a disciple that could have done much good on earth and inherited "riches in heaven." We never hear of this rich young ruler again. That is a sad story, one that, unfortunately, is replayed over and over again in our day. The words of the Savior, given in a different context and under different circumstances, serve as the moral, if you will, of this story. The characters may change, but the message remains the same: "For what is a man profited, if he shall gain the whole world, and lose his own soul?" (Matthew 16:26).

WHERE MUCH IS GIVEN, MUCH IS REQUIRED

There is yet another episode in the Savior's life which serves as a living sermon for us concerning the necessity of possessing a proper perspective on wealth. There was a publican, a tax collector from Jericho named Zacchaeus. In fact, he was the chief, or supervisor, of all of the tax collectors in that region and a very wealthy man. When Jesus passed through Jericho, Zacchaeus went out to see and hear the Master. Because the crowds pressed around Jesus, Zacchaeus could not get near the Lord, "because he was little of stature" (Luke 19:3). So this prominent and prosperous man climbed up in a sycamore tree so that he could behold the Son of God and hear his words.

"And when Jesus came to the place, he looked up, and saw him, and said unto him, Zacchaeus, make haste, and come down; for to day I must abide at thy house.

"And he made haste, and came down, and received him joyfully.

"And when they saw it, they all murmured, saying, That he was gone to be guest with a man that is a sinner.

"And Zacchaeus stood, and said unto the Lord; Behold, Lord, the half of my goods I give to the poor; and if I have taken any thing from any man by false accusation, I restore him fourfold.

"And Jesus said unto him, This day is salvation come to this house, forsomuch as he also is a son of Abraham" (Luke 19:5–9).

What a contrast to the rich young ruler, who was devout in

keeping the commandments but could not give his all to the Lord because he was possessed by his possessions. In contrast, Zacchaeus, as a publican, was despised by the people of the land and viewed as a vile sinner—because of his occupation, not because of the spiritual quality of his life. What others could not see, Jesus could. Zacchaeus believed in the Lord, desired salvation, and sought to be a disciple. Salvation—"the unsearchable riches of Christ"—could come to him because he was not possessed by his possessions. He did not put his trust and devotion in riches— he willingly gave half of all that he had to those who had little. The scriptural record is silent concerning what becomes of Zacchaeus. I am impressed, however, with his faith and devotion, his compassion and charity, his understanding of the proper use of earthly riches, and their relative insignificance compared to the riches of eternity. Zacchaeus, like many other devout disciples, such as Joseph of Arimathea, had obtained wealth, but not at the expense of the things of God. His loyalty was undivided. His priorities were right. He epitomized what Jesus taught concerning the proper priorities that are required of disciples. "Seek not the things of this world but seek ye first to build up the kingdom of God, and to establish his righteousness, and all these things shall be added unto you" (JST Matthew 6:38).

"Seek not for riches but for wisdom," the Living Christ declared in the dispensation of the fulness of times, "and, behold, the mysteries of God shall be unfolded unto you, and then shall you be made rich. Behold, he that hath eternal life is rich" (D&C 11:7). Seeking the riches of the world is not the way to salvation. Seeking the wisdom of God, keeping the commandments, and striving for eternal life, however, will inevitably bring prosperity and an enhanced quality of life. But that does not mean that we will all be blessed with riches in this life. We will, however, be blessed. And with the blessings come responsibilities. "For unto whomsoever much is given, of him shall be much required," the Savior taught (Luke 12:48).

The Book of Mormon prophet Jacob chastised his own people for their worldliness and lust for wealth. It was not riches he condemned, but the people's tendency, when they obtained riches, to become puffed up in pride and diverted from seeking the riches of eternity. Thus, in the end, their riches cankered their souls. "Before ye seek for riches, seek ye for the kingdom of God" was his admonishment. "And after ye have obtained a hope in Christ ye shall obtain riches, if ye seek them; *and ye will seek them for the intent to do good—to clothe the naked, and to feed the hungry, and to liberate the captive, and administer relief to the sick and the afflicted*" (Jacob 2:18–19; emphasis added). Commenting on this passage, Elder L. Tom Perry of the Quorum of the Twelve Apostles taught: "So often it is the order of things that is fundamental in the Lord's instructions to us. The Lord is not telling us that we should not be prosperous. This would be inconsistent with the many records we have of Him blessing His people with prosperity. But He is telling us that we should seek prosperity only after we have sought and found Him. Then, because our hearts are right, because we love Him first and foremost, we will choose to invest the riches we obtain in building His kingdom."[12]

Perhaps there is nothing better to help us keep our eternal perspective about what things matter most and to keep us from being choked by the cares and riches of the world, than to "administer of [our] substance unto him that standeth in need" (Mosiah 4:16; see also verses 19–27). No matter what our own unique financial circumstances—no matter our abundance or our needs—we can show the Lord that we love him more than money and that we will serve his cause more than mammon. We show that love by how we use our means.

When our children were young they would often ask, "Daddy, are we rich?" At first I would laugh at their question and think to myself, "I am a poor teacher. How can they think we are rich? Haven't they noticed the junker car we drive? Don't they see how little we can afford?" I couldn't in clear conscience say, "No children, we are poor as church mice." So I mustered the best response I could come up with at the time: "Yes, children, we are rich—rich in blessings!" That has become a classic statement in our family lore. Whenever we have to say, "We can't afford that!" or "We don't have enough money for this!" they inevitably come back with, "But at least we are rich in blessings!" O, how true! Whenever I feel sorry for myself, thinking I can't afford something that I think I need (or at least "just want"), I think of the people I have seen in various parts of the world who have so little and yet are so happy! We are indeed rich in blessings! Serving mammon, however, causes us to feel we are poor, no matter how much we have. Serving God and putting him first in our lives reminds us how rich we truly are—no matter how little or how much we possess. Feeling "rich in blessings" should cause our hearts to be drawn out in compassion for others. As one of my favorite hymns declares:

> Because I have been given much, I too must give;
> Because of thy great bounty, Lord, each day I live
> I shall divide my gifts from thee
> With every brother that I see
> Who has the need of help from me.
>
> Because I have been sheltered, fed by thy good care,
> I cannot see another's lack and I not share
> My glowing fire, my loaf of bread
> My roof's safe shelter overhead,
> That he too may be comforted.
>
> Because I have been blessed by thy great love, dear Lord,
> I'll share thy love again, according to thy word.

I shall give love to those in need;
I'll show that love by word and deed:
Thus shall my thanks be thanks indeed.[13]

To keep our eyes on the riches of eternity, the Lord has given us responsibility and ample opportunity to give to those in need. "The more we are blessed with means, the more we are blessed with responsibility," President Brigham Young taught. "The more we are blessed with wisdom and ability, the more we are placed under the necessity of using that wisdom and ability in the spread of righteousness, the subjugation of sin and misery, and the amelioration of the condition of mankind. The man that has only one talent and the man that has five talents have responsibility accordingly. *If we have a world of means, we have a world of responsibility.*"[14] Speaking for himself, he further declared: "If I have wealth and cannot use it to the glory of God and the building up of His kingdom, I ask the Lord to take it from me."[15]

Each of us, although we are as beggars before the Lord, is rich in blessings and, thus, rich with responsibility to give. In giving we lose ourselves from the oppressive bands of greediness, self-centeredness, and living a life of self-gratification. Giving liberally of our means, as God has liberally given to us, liberates us from the pull of the things of the world. For some, giving may occur in the form of substantial sums. For others, our gifts may be small. But remember, the widow's mite may be just as great proportionally as the contributions of the wealthy. Each of us has a responsibility. If I cannot give of my monetary means, I can give of my time and talent. I may not be able to donate property or money to build a temple, but I can serve there. I can pay fast offerings. I can serve on the Church farm. I can donate time in the cannery. There is so much that can be done and so many ways to give. I may not be able to do all things, but I can do some things. I cannot give as much as I would like, but I can give something. And with each gift of means to those in need—whether that gift be of money, time, talent, love, service, kindness, friendship—the things of the world and all the toys money can buy will not seem quite so attractive, quite so necessary, or quite so important. When we finally abandon our chase after the mirage of materialism—when we come to realize that living what the world calls the "good life" is a *shadow* and living "God's life" is *substance*—we will find real riches.

"You cannot serve God and mammon," Jesus declared. Well, then, who will you and I serve? For what will we give our lives? To what cause are we giving our souls—seeking stuff or easing suffering? Are we seeking first and foremost for a lasting legacy of love and righteousness for our families, or are we just leaving them things that, like old Christmas toys, wear out, lose their appeal, and are abandoned in closets and attics? Are we like the rich young ruler, who turned his back on the Lord—rich, but sad—or Zacchaeus the publican, who loved the Lord with his whole soul, loved his fellowmen, blessed the poor with his means, and found salvation? Choose you this day whom you will serve—mammon or the Master.

Notes

1. Brigham Young, *Discourses of Brigham Young*, sel. John A. Widtsoe (Salt Lake City: Deseret Book, 1954), 306.

2. Ezra Taft Benson, in Conference Report, April 1988, 59.

3. Harold B. Lee, in *The Teachings of Harold B. Lee*, ed. by Clyde J. Williams (Salt Lake City: Bookcraft, 1996), 328–29; emphasis added.

4. Ezra Taft Benson, in *The Teachings of Ezra Taft Benson* (Salt Lake City: Bookcraft, 1988), 475.

5. Spencer W. Kimball, *The Teachings of Spencer W. Kimball*, ed. Edward L. Kimball (Salt Lake City: Bookcraft, 1982), 353.

6. Brigham Young, *Discourses of Brigham Young*, 314.

7. Ibid., 314–15.

8. Neal A. Maxwell, *All These Things Shall Give Thee Experience* (Salt Lake City: Deseret Book, 1979), 61.

9. Joseph B. Wirthlin, "The Straight and Narrow Way," *Ensign*, November 1990, 65.

10. Brigham Young, *Journal of Discourses*, 26 vols. (London: Latter-day Saints' Book Depot, 1854–86), 13:280.

11. Brigham Young, *Discourses of Brigham Young,* 315.

12. L. Tom Perry, in Conference Report, April 1987, 40.

13. Grace Noll Crowell, in *Hymns of The Church of Jesus Christ of Latter-day Saints* (Salt Lake City: The Church of Jesus Christ of Latter-day Saints, 1985), no. 219. Copyright 1936 by Harper & Row, Publishers, Inc. Copyright © renewed 1964 by Grace Noll Crowell. Reprinted by permission of HarperCollins Publishers Inc.

14. Brigham Young, *Discourses of Brigham Young,* 315; emphasis added.

15. Brigham Young, *Journal of Discourses,* 13:280.

CHAPTER 7

TAKING UP THE CROSS

When I taught seminary in Arizona, I showed a Church film to the students entitled *And Should We Die*. The movie is based on a true story about Latter-day Saints in Mexico who were persecuted for their religious beliefs by Zapatista rebels during the Mexican civil war shortly after the turn of the twentieth century. The movie focuses primarily on two LDS fathers, the branch president and his first counselor, who were imprisoned and sentenced to death. They were told they would be spared the firing squad if they would denounce their Mormon beliefs. Because they refused to do so, the two men, President Rafael Monroy and Brother Vicente Morales, were executed in front of their families and branch members on 17 July 1915.

My students were deeply affected by the movie; many were even in tears. In this setting I asked my sobered high school students—whose minds only minutes before had been on such things as proms, football games, cool cars, hot guys, and what they were going to do for fun on the weekend—"Would you be willing to lay down your life rather than denounce your faith and testimony of the restored gospel?" The question was designed to get the students to appreciate the sacrifices others had made for the gospel's sake. It was also meant to stimulate self-examination of their convictions and commitments to the Lord. I didn't expect anyone to answer. And, at first, only an outspoken macho young man on the back row said anything. He boldly declared, "Yeah, I'd be willing to die for the Lord." I wasn't sure that he was serious, because he was rarely serious about anything. However, this time he seemed very sincere. After a moment or two of dead silence, others began earnestly and in hushed tones (rare in a high school seminary class) to declare their willingness to die for the cause of the Master. A young woman with tears streaming down her face sweetly stated that she, too, would be willing to die for her beliefs, "because Jesus suffered and died for me." It was one of the most remarkable occasions in my teaching career.

The moment I shall never forget, however, came after the bell rang to end our class. As the students were filing out of the class-room, one young man turned back to me and quietly asked, "Brother Top, would you die for him?" I hadn't been expecting that, so a moment or two of silence passed that seemed like an eternity. I was so flustered I didn't really know quite how to answer. Before I could answer, he turned and left the building. I have thought of that moment many times since. I have replayed it over and over in my mind, each time giving a response that I thought would adequately and profoundly declare my devotion to the Lord and his kingdom. Yet the young man never got an answer from me. I know what I should have said and what I wanted to say. But what would I really say—and more important, what would I do—when my life and soul depended on the answer?

I like to believe that I could definitively and without hesita-tion declare that I would gladly lay down my life for my faith. Yet I am not sure giving that answer is as easy as it sounds. In fact, I am quite convinced that it isn't that easy—nor was true disciple-ship ever intended to be easy, comfortable, convenient, painless, or free from sacrifice and sorrow. Nevertheless, I hope that I could and would be able to sacrifice my life for my testimony. In the meantime, however, I can say (as I should have said to my student who posed that penetrating question to me), "I have made a covenant to do so if necessary." To follow Christ with "full purpose of heart" and to be a determined disciple in the truest sense of the word requires a faith and commitment that comes only from a willingness to lay one's all on the altar of God. To those who desired to be disciples of Christ, Jesus repeatedly declared: "If any man will come after me, let him deny himself, and *take up his cross* daily, and follow me" (Luke 9:23; emphasis added. See also Matthew 10:38; 16:24; Mark 8:34; 10:21). What does it mean to "take up the cross"? The scriptures seem to indicate that the phrase has a double meaning, affecting both *life* and *death*. Taking up the cross means that disciples must (1) be willing to suffer and *die* as martyrs for the cause of Christ, and (2) be willing to continually *live* the life of a true and faithful follower of the Savior.

TAKING UP THE CROSS OF CHRIST: SYMBOL OF THE ULTIMATE SACRIFICE

All Christians recognize the cross as a graphic symbol of the Crucifixion—the horrible agony and suffering the Lord endured at the hands of his Roman executioners. Crucifixion may have been perfected by the Romans, but it certainly didn't begin with them. For many centuries and by many different nations and cultures, crucifixion in various forms had been practiced as a means of torture and execution. The Greek word from which the word *crucifixion* is translated in our scriptures is *stauros*, which literally refers to a stake or pole upon which the victim was fastened in some cruel and torturous manner. Crucifixion was designed not only to bring about a slow and agonizing death but was also a form of extreme humiliation. Prior to the actual execution, the condemned man would be stripped naked, scourged, mocked, and forced to carry the cross beam to the place of execution through a midst of jeering spectators. Death by crucifixion was intended to send a signal to society that the "criminal" condemned for treason and sedition was beneath contempt—the lowest of the low.

The phrase "to take up one's cross" was a popular saying in

Jesus' day that may have originated with the zealots and other nationalists who worked to overturn Roman occupation of their land.[1] Those who took up the cross were willing to give their lives for their convictions and the cause of freedom. The Savior taught his listeners that *his* cause—the liberation promised through his atonement and gospel teachings—was an even greater cause than this and was one that believers should be willing to die for to defend and uphold. Taking up the cross came to mean the sacrifice of everything, including one's life if necessary, as well as being willing to endure persecution, humiliation, and the mockery of the world for one's convictions. It is this kind of faith, commitment, and willingness to sacrifice all that the Book of Mormon prophet Jacob spoke when he declared: "But, behold, the righteous, the saints of the Holy One of Israel, they who have believed in the Holy One of Israel, *they who have endured the crosses of the world, and despised the shame of it*, they shall inherit the kingdom of God, which was prepared for them from the foundation of the world, and their joy shall be full forever" (2 Nephi 9:18; emphasis added).

Taking up the cross means the same thing for us today as it did for the ancient disciples. "And he that will not take up his cross and follow me, and keep my commandments," the Lord declared in this dispensation, "the same shall not be saved" (D&C 56:2). Discipleship requires a devotion and allegiance to the Lord that allows nothing—not property or prestige, family or friends—to be more important to us than the Savior and his cause. "He that loveth father or mother more than me is not worthy of me: and he that loveth son or daughter more than me is not worthy of me," Jesus declared. "And he that taketh not his cross, and followeth after me, is not worthy of me" (Matthew 10:37–38). President Harold B. Lee testified: "I bear witness that until a person has been willing to sacrifice all he possesses in the world, not even withholding his own life if it were necessary for the upbuilding of the kingdom, then only can he claim kinship to Him who gave His life that men might be."[2]

Just as all ancient sacrifices were but "a similitude of the sacrifice of the Only Begotten of the Father, which is full of grace and truth" (Moses 5:7), taking up the cross today and any sacrifice associated with that discipleship is also a similitude of the sacrifice of the Only Begotten. And, because of his sacrifice, all we sacrifice in true faith for him will be restored unto us and crowned with celestial glory.

LIVING FOR THE LORD:
TAKING UP THE CROSS THROUGH DAILY DISCIPLESHIP

As I have pondered President Lee's statement and the deep significance of the need to take up one's cross, I have wondered if I am truly willing to lay down my life and my all for the Lord. As I struggle with this issue, one thought seems to settle upon my mind and in my heart. It is as if I can hear the voice of the Savior saying, "I don't need you to *die* for me. I need you to *live* for me." It seems simple; but it is deeply profound. Living for the Lord is in many ways far more demanding and a greater test of faith than dying for the Lord. It is this sentiment that is reflected in the apostle Paul's admonition to the Roman Saints: "Present your bodies a *living sacrifice*" (Romans 12:1; emphasis added).

Clearly, the cross is a symbol of death, but so is it the ultimate symbol of life. Taking up the cross requires not only a willingness to sacrifice and even die for the Lord, but also to live and love as the Lord did. Taking up the cross is also a symbol of sacrifice. Rather than a sacrifice of life and limb, however, it is often symbolic of self-sacrifice—a sacrifice of sinfulness and selfishness—a sacrifice of the natural man and all ways and things of the world that prevent consecrated discipleship.

Various accounts of Jesus' teachings to take up the cross denote a double meaning of *death* and *life*. Luke, for example, adds an important word in his account that clearly bespeaks *living for the Lord*. "If any man will come after me, let him deny himself, *and take up his cross daily*, and follow me" (Luke 9:23; emphasis added). The word *daily* makes all the difference. Laying down your life—*dying for the Lord*—can be done only once. Taking up the cross, however, is to be done daily. *Living for the Lord* is an act of daily discipleship and devotion. How do we take up the cross every day? The answer is found in the same scriptural accounts. In addition to the word *daily*, Luke (and the other Gospel writers) highlights the Savior's use of the phrases "deny himself" and "follow me." What do we deny ourselves and how do we follow the Lord? The Joseph Smith Translation provides the answer, "And now for a man to take up his cross, is to *deny himself all ungodliness, and every worldly lust, and keep my commandments*" (JST Matthew 16:26; emphasis added).

What we sacrifice, or deny ourselves, in taking up the cross is the ungodliness of the world. As Elder Neal A. Maxwell insightfully observed, "So it is that real, personal sacrifice never was placing an animal on the altar. Instead, it is a willingness to put the animal in us upon the altar and letting it be consumed!"[3] It is this kind of sacrifice, this kind of self-denial, that constitutes *living for the Lord*. This kind of "taking up the cross" must be continual, not episodic. It means, as Jesus declared, that we must "forsake the world, and save your souls" (JST Matthew 16:29).

The phrase "taking up the cross," as it describes the need for continual faith and devotion, may be linked to something else Jesus taught. "Take my yoke upon you," he declared (Matthew 11:29). It is interesting to note that the Greek word for yoke is *zugos*, which implies a beam or pole that attaches or connects two things together. A cross beam, to which a condemned man was attached and required to carry to his crucifixion, could also be referred to as a yoke. Some Bible scholars have suggested that the phrases "take up the cross" and "take my yoke" are conceptually related to each other.[4] Did Jesus use the phrases interchangeably? We do not know, but it is interesting to ponder the wordplay and the images created by the metaphors.

The Jews of Jesus' day often used the term *yoke* to refer to the "burden of the law"—their connection to and responsibility to live the law of Moses. They were under "the yoke of the law." It was, as it were, the *cross* they had to bear. Many viewed that yoke as harsh or burdensome. Those who felt that way did not realize that it was the yoke that connected or attached them to their God. Jesus was offering to exchange yokes with them—inviting them to give up the old yoke of the Mosiac law and take up the new yoke—his way or "burden."[5] The law of Christ—the higher law, the everlasting gospel of Jesus Christ—fulfilled and superseded the law of Moses. It is this yoke that Jesus described as easy.

"Come unto me, all ye that labour and are heavy laden, and I will give you rest.

"Take my yoke upon you, and learn of me; for I am meek and lowly in heart: and ye shall find rest unto your souls.

"For my yoke is easy, and my burden is light" (Matthew 11:28–30).

The word *yoke*, or the "burden of the law," reminded the ancient Jews of their covenantal obligations. In this sense, taking up the cross or taking Christ's yoke upon us is the same—a reminder that discipleship requires responsibilities as well as sacrifices—living as well as dying for the faith. Taking the Savior's yoke upon us causes us to become connected, fastened, or attached to him. This is no passive endeavor. It requires all of our being—heart, might, mind, and soul. Certainly that is what Jesus meant when he taught us that taking up the cross requires following him—not just following him in death, but following his example, becoming connected to his gospel and securely fastened to his atoning sacrifice. Taking up the cross in that sense requires continual effort and obedience, daily devotion and diligence, and recurring repentance and recommitment when we fall short. Dying as a martyr for our faith in Christ may be an event, but taking up the cross of Christ as a true disciple is a process. The process of discipleship begins with our *choosing* to follow the Master and taking his yoke or cross upon us. It ends (in reality it never ends, but you know what I mean) with total *consecration* of ourselves to him and his kingdom.

These two—*choice* and *consecration*—are like bookends in the process of discipleship with two more phases of discipleship located between them—*conviction* and *conversion*. Taking the cross of Christ upon us and remaining yoked with him provides passage through each phase. Only at the end of the process, however, does the yoke become truly easy and the burden really light. At the end of the "discipleship tunnel" is found genuine light and life, peace and joy inexpressible. To attain those we must take up the cross, not lay it down or abandon it—remaining in the yoke, fastened securely to the Savior. True discipleship requires nothing less.

CONVINCED: WHAT YOU KNOW

Many people *chose* to listen to Jesus—some out of sincere faith, others out of sheer curiosity. Many followed the Master from place to place. Yet that didn't make them followers of the Lord, in the truest sense of the word. Many witnessed his miracles and were amazed. Yet that didn't make them disciples. Perhaps many even felt spiritual awakening within their souls when they heard Jesus speak "as one having authority from God" (JST Matthew 7:37). Nonetheless, more was required of those who became devoted disciples and true believers. It is the same for us today. After choosing to listen, observe, and feel what Jesus has to offer, true disciples must become *convinced* of his divinity as the literal Son of God and the Savior and Redeemer of the world, as well as the truthfulness of his gospel.

"Whom say ye that I am?" Jesus asked the Twelve (Matthew 16:15). His question remains relevant to any and all who desire to become a disciple. Answers such as the following, though each is true, are inadequate and miss the essence of what it means to be his disciple.

> "You are a great teacher! Your teachings make a lot of sense. I especially like your parables."

> "You are a miracle worker! I am impressed with how you can make the blind see."

> "You are a good person! You are so kind and loving to others."

In response to the Master's probing question, Peter declared: "Thou art the Christ, the Son of the living God" (Matthew 16:16). Peter had *chosen* to leave his fishing boat when Jesus said, "Come, follow me." No doubt he had been impressed with the Savior's miracles and had been inspired and instructed by his teaching. However, the real staying power of Peter's discipleship did not begin with those moments, but rather when he became *convinced*, when he had a testimony that burned within his soul. As Jesus declared: "Flesh and blood hath not revealed it unto thee, but my Father which is in heaven" (Matthew 16:17). This *conviction*—this witness that comes by the power of the Holy Ghost—is available to all. It is a requisite first step in taking up the cross of Christ.

It requires considerable diligence, intellectually and spiritually, to obtain a personal *conviction* of the truth. That is one reason why there were many, many more people who "followed" Jesus, listened to his sermons, witnessed his miracles, and felt of his love, than those who *truly* followed him, valiantly remaining with him until the end—and beyond. Disciples that have come to know with certainty who he really is are those who have continuously and seriously studied his words (and those of his servants), have pondered them, and have prayed for a witness of the truth through the power of the Holy Ghost.

It is interesting to me to note that the pattern of discipleship—of taking up the cross—is evidenced by the progression of questions in the temple recommend interview. The first few all deal with this step in the process we call *conviction*—what we *know*. "Do you have a testimony of God the Father and his Son, Jesus Christ, and the Holy Ghost?" "Do you have a testimony of the Atonement and of Jesus' role as Savior and Redeemer of the world?" Before any question is asked about behavior and worthiness, we report on our level of *conviction*—our personal testimony and spiritual knowledge of truth. Before we are asked concerning what we are *doing* (or not doing) in our lives, we are asked about what we *know*. Yet, *knowing* and *doing* are interrelated. They are not, nor can they be, independent and separable in the lives of true disciples. "My doctrine is not mine, but his that sent me," Jesus taught. "If any man will *do* his will, he shall *know* of the doctrine, whether it be of God, or whether I speak of myself" (John 7:16–17; emphasis added).

Keeping the commandments and doing one's duty in the Church are essential elements for gaining a personal testimony. "I know, too, that a knowledge of the truth of the gospel may be obtained only through obedience to the principles thereof," President David O. McKay taught. "In other words, the best way to know the truth of any principle is to live it."[6] President McKay often recounted that his own personal testimony came, not in some dramatic or mystical manner, but "as a natural sequence to the performance of duty."[7] In this manner, *doing* can lead to *knowing*. In turn, *conviction* can lead to *conversion*. This personal conviction—this "assurance of the reality, truth, and goodness of God, [and] of the teachings and Atonement of Jesus Christ"[8]—coupled with *conversion* enables and empowers a disciple to take upon him the yoke of Christ—that yoke of discipleship with all its attendant responsibilities and requirements. With *conviction* leading to *conversion*, that yoke—the cross of Christ—truly becomes easy to bear.

CONVERTED:
WHAT YOU DO

"If ye *know* these things," Jesus declared, "happy are ye if ye *do* them" (John 13:17; emphasis added). Taking up the cross of Christ—becoming and remaining a true disciple of the Master—requires both spiritual knowledge of his divinity *and* obedience to his gospel. Testimony has no saving power if it doesn't lead to greater righteousness, deeper devotion to God, and increased service to our fellowmen. The spiritual witness of truth is important, but it is only a beginning point. *Conviction* must lead to *conversion*—the willing submission to the principles and ordinances of the gospel and faithful, not blind, obedience to the teachings of the Lord and his servants.

"Not every one that saith unto me, Lord, Lord, shall enter into the kingdom of heaven," Jesus taught, "*but he that doeth the will of my Father*" (Matthew 7:21; emphasis added). Perhaps we can paraphrase this verse to illustrate the progression from knowledge to action—*conviction* to *conversion*—that is required of true disciples. Not everyone that has a testimony and says, "I know that Jesus is the Christ" or "I know that the gospel is true" will inherit the celestial kingdom. Those who gain a spiritual witness of truth and then faithfully seek to live in accordance with that spiritual knowledge—those who *know and do* what the Lord says—will be exalted. A convert is not just a person who gains a knowledge of truth, but one who then fully embraces that truth and seeks to live it. One cannot really take up the cross with intellectual effort alone, no matter how strong the conviction. Conversion must follow, or the disciple will eventually stumble under the weight of the cross and detach himself from the yoke of the gospel.

Many years ago, Sister Naomi Randall wrote the familiar Primary song, "I Am a Child of God." In her original version (which I remember from my own days in Primary), the words of the chorus were:

> *Lead me, guide me, walk beside me,*
> *Help me find the way.*
> *Teach me all that I must know*
> *To live with Him someday.*[9]

President Spencer W. Kimball suggested that the word *know* should be changed to *do*—and that is how we sing the song today. He wanted children of God of all ages to understand that knowing is important, but only as it leads us to doing what we must do to someday dwell with our Father in Heaven. Each time I sing this familiar hymn I am reminded of the dual demands of discipleship—knowing and doing, conviction and conversion. The scriptures, both ancient and modern, repeatedly remind us of this. "No man can come unto me," the Savior said, "except he *doeth the will of my Father who hath sent me*" (JST John 6:65; emphasis added). To the Nephites, the resurrected Lord likewise stated, "For that which ye have seen me *do* even that shall ye *do*" (3 Nephi 27:21; emphasis added). And in this dispensation, he declared, "He that receiveth my law [obtains a spiritual witness of the truthfulness of the gospel] and *doeth* it, the same is my disciple; and he that saith he receiveth it and *doeth* it not, the same is not my disciple, and shall be cast out from among you" (D&C 41:5; emphasis added).

This connection between knowing and doing is clearly illustrated in the temple recommend interview. After the first questions regarding testimony and *conviction* are addressed, then we are evaluated in our manner of behavior and obedience. What we *do* speaks somewhat of the degree of our discipleship and our conversion. "*Do* you keep the Word of Wisdom?" "*Do* you live the law of chastity?" "*Do* you pay a full tithing?" and so on. These actions are important indicators of our commitment and conversion. They are like mile markers along the pathway of discipleship, but they do not, nor can they by themselves, tell the whole story. Outward actions—*what we do*—may tell much about the direction we are heading. In reality, however, it is our heart and inner spirituality and commitment—*what we are*—that ultimately guides us to the desired destination. Taking up the cross requires *knowing* and *doing*, but most of all, it requires *being*. In fact, we are not completely converted until our whole being is positively changed and we become "new creatures in Christ."

CONSECRATED:
WHAT YOU ARE

The teachings of the Savior clearly indicate that knowing and doing, as essential as they are, do not fully constitute discipleship. "Many will say to me in that day, Lord, Lord, have we not prophesied in thy name? and in thy name have we cast out devils? and in thy name done many wonderful works?" (Matthew 7:22). The capstone characteristic of taking his yoke upon us is becoming *consecrated*—giving ourselves and our hearts (not just our minds and our actions) wholly to his cause—striving to *become* more like the Savior in all aspects of our lives, both inwardly and outwardly. In this manner, taking up the cross is not just what we *know* and how we *behave*, but what we have *become*—what we really *are* through and through. "Some give of their time yet withhold themselves, being present without giving of their presence," Elder Neal A. Maxwell eloquently stated, "going through the superficial motions of membership instead of the deep emotions of consecrated discipleship. . . .

"Real disciples are . . . precept by precept and experience by experience, *becoming* ever more like the Master they serve."[10]

Elder Dallin H. Oaks explained the process in this manner:

"The Apostle Paul taught that the Lord's teachings and teachers were given that we may all attain 'the measure of the stature of the fulness of Christ' (Eph. 4:13). This process requires far more than acquiring knowledge. It is not even enough for us to be *convinced* of the gospel; we must act and think so that we are *converted* by it. In contrast to the institutions of the world, which teach us to *know* something, the gospel of Jesus Christ challenges us to *become* something.

". . . The Final Judgment is not just an evaluation of a sum total of good and evil acts—what we have *done*. It is an acknowledgment of the final effect of our acts and thoughts—what we have *become*. It is not enough for anyone just to go through the motions. The commandments, ordinances, and covenants of the gospel are not a list of deposits required to be made in some heavenly account. The gospel of Jesus Christ is a plan that shows us how to become what our Heavenly Father desires us to become."[11]

Building upon the analogy I've used before, we see the culmination of this process in the final question of the temple interview. "*Are you worthy* to enter the temple and participate in temple ordinances?" I find a striking parallel between these questions and the process by which we take up the cross. What do we *know*? What do we *do* (or how do we *behave*)? What *are* we? Each phase—knowing, doing, and becoming—shapes the man and woman of Christ. Being, however, is the ultimate indicator of our devotion as disciples.

The Lord doesn't just want us to know where the meeting-house is; he wants us to attend services there. Attending, however, must be more than just staying awake or even answering a few questions in quorums or classes. It is not enough to just go through the Church, we must have the Church—its ordinances, practices, teachings—go through us and become a very real part of us. We must live the gospel, but also make it our life. The Lord doesn't just want us to be active and fulfill our duties; he wants us to come to truly worship him, know him, and be drawn to him and his ways. He wants us not only to follow him and do his works, but to become like him. Being a consecrated disciple—taking up his cross—will cause me to not only avoid evil influences and immoral thoughts and behaviors, but to become a man of virtue. Virtue is not just a matter of what we do or don't do; it's a matter of what we are. The Lord doesn't want us simply to be quiet in church and act in a reverent manner; he wants us to be reverent. Reverence is not only what we do or how we act, but it is also what we are— people whose hearts are filled with love, adoration, and awe for the things of God. The Lord doesn't want me to merely *go* to the temple; he wants me to *be* a temple—to *become* the kind of person where the Spirit of the Lord can dwell in abundance. Conviction requires my mind and spirit. Conversion requires my best behavior, strict obedience, and devotion to duty. Consecration, however, requires all of this and so much more. It requires all of me—my whole soul. "And now, my beloved brethren [and sisters], I would that ye should come unto Christ, who is the Holy One of Israel. . . . Yea, come unto him, and *offer your whole souls as an offering unto him*" (Omni 1:26; emphasis added).

"As I Have Loved You"

Perhaps you are asking, as I have asked myself many times throughout the years, "How do I become that kind of consecrated disciple? How can I get from knowing and doing to being?" Unfortunately (or fortunately, for our sakes), there is no checklist of things to be done and crossed off, no detailed, sequential flowchart to guide us, no recipe card of ingredients and directions to be meticulously followed. There are some things, however, that I do know we need to do. There are some steps, if you will, that can be followed. I know what needs to be done to obtain and retain a testimony—becoming *convinced*. I know what I must *do* to keep the commandments and fulfill my covenantal responsibilities—

becoming *converted*. This much of taking up the cross I can do of myself. The becoming totally *consecrated*—becoming like the Savior—requires something and someone else.

At the Last Supper, Jesus taught the Twelve: "A new commandment I give unto you, That ye love one another; as I have loved you, that ye also love one another." Then comes this familiar, yet profound declaration: "By this shall all men know that ye are my disciples, if ye have love one to another" (John 13:34–35). I think the answer to our question, "How do we *become* consecrated disciples of Christ?" is found in that statement. The *something* that allows us to *become* his disciples is love. The *Someone* who enables us to carry the cross with complete consecration is Christ himself.

I don't think Jesus was saying that the hallmark of true discipleship is based only on how we treat each other or serve our fellowmen. The key phrase seems to be "as I have loved you." His love—*charity,* or *the pure love of* Christ—is that which makes all the difference. His atoning sacrifice—the ultimate act of charity—is that which transforms us. We *choose* him, but he *changes* us. Partaking of his atonement is like yeast in the bread-making process. We can provide the ingredients—the efforts and diligence to come to *know,* the obedience and keeping the commandments that helps us become *converted*—but he, like the yeast, raises us into consecrated disciples. In this manner, the hallmark of discipleship is love—his love. When we have come to taste of that love which is "most desirable above all things" (see 1 Nephi 8:10–12; 11:16–22), bearing the yoke of Christ truly becomes easy and burdens become light. His love for us affects everything we think, everything we know, everything we do.

When we are transformed by his love, it becomes easy to live his commandments. It becomes easy to love and serve one another—not because of what we do, but because of what he has made of us. The phrase "as I have loved you" has come to mean to me "because I have loved you." Because he has loved me, I am filled with his love. Because of this pure love, taking up his cross daily is not a chore, it is a privilege. His yoke is not a burden, it is a blessing. Daily partaking of his love through faith, repentance, and obedience to the principles and ordinances of his gospel will inevitably transform us from merely *knowing* and *doing* to *being* consecrated disciples. In this manner, carrying the cross of Christ will not weigh us down but lift us up.

Now, more than two decades since my teaching days in Arizona, I still think of that lone student asking me as he was exiting my seminary class, "Brother Top, would you die for Christ?" I believe I now know the answer: "Only if I am daily living for him." It is those daily acts of *conviction, conversion,* and *consecration*—the degree to which I am living for him—that will determine whether or not I could really die for him. There is one thing I know for sure: The more I come to know, feel, and experience the transforming power of the Atonement, the more I desire to love him, the more I desire to serve him, and the more I feel to give to him. Even dying for him seems too small a sacrifice. As the noted hymn writer, Isaac Watts, penned:

> *When I survey the wondrous cross*
> *On which the Prince of glory died,*
> *My richest gain I count but loss,*
> *And pour contempt on all my pride.*
>
> *Forbid it, Lord, that I should boast,*
> *Save in the death of Christ, my God;*
> *All the vain things that charm me most,*
> *I sacrifice them to his blood.*
>
> *See from his head, his hands, his feet,*
> *Sorrow and love flow mingled down;*
> *Did e'er such love and sorrow meet,*
> *Or thorns compose so rich a crown?*

Were the whole realm of nature mine,
That were a present far too small:
Love so amazing, so divine,
Demands my soul, my life, my all.[12]

Notes

1. See Gehrard Friedrich, ed., *Theological Dictionary of the New Testament*, trans. Geoffrey W. Bromiley (Grand Rapids, Mich.: Eerdmans Publishing, 1971), 7:572–84.
2. Harold B. Lee, in Conference Report, October 1965, 131.
3. Neal A. Maxwell, in Conference Report, April 1995, 91.
4. See Friedrich, *Theological Dictionary*, 7:578.
5. See *The Interpreter's Bible*, ed. George Arthur Buttrick, 12 vols. (New York: Abingdon Press, 1952), 7:390–91.
6. David O. McKay, *Cherished Experiences from the Writings of David O. McKay*, comp. Clare Middlemiss (Salt Lake City: Deseret Book, 1976), 16.
7. Ibid., 7.
8. *Encyclopedia of Mormonism*, 4 vols., ed. Daniel H. Ludlow (New York: Macmillan, 1992), 4:1470.
9. See Naomi W. Randall, "I Am a Child of God," *Hymns of The Church of Jesus Christ of Latter-day Saints* (Salt Lake City: The Church of Jesus Christ of Latter-day Saints, 1985), no. 301.
10. Neal A. Maxwell, in Conference Report, April 1987, 87.
11. Dallin H. Oaks, "The Challenge to Become," *Ensign*, November 2000, 32.
12. Isaac Watts, *Hymns and Spiritual Songs* (n.p., 1707).

CHAPTER 8

"WILL YE ALSO GO AWAY?"

Across from my desk sat a young man with pain in his countenance. "What if it is not true?" he asked me over and over again. "What if the Church really isn't the true church and I have wasted all this time?" I was his priesthood leader and had been working with him for several months. He had his share of doubts and questions, but that wasn't the whole problem. He had previously been disciplined by the Church for conduct unbecoming a Latter-day Saint. I was trying to help him in his quest to regain full fellowship in the Church. What he needed to do and become in his life through the process of sincere repentance had been clearly articulated by the disciplinary council. He had made some progress, but was not yet fully repentant or in a spiritual condition to regain full Church privileges. As I explained to him that I was not inclined to reconvene the disciplinary council and thus reinstate him into full fellowship, he responded: "Well, I guess that's best since I am not sure that the Church is even true. I'm not sure that I even want to continue as a member." I was somewhat taken aback. Just a moment earlier he had almost been demanding (or at least pleading with) me to reconvene a disciplinary council so he could be, what he characterized as, "a full member of the Church."

I was puzzled by his comments. Why would his Church membership be so important to him one moment and virtually insignificant the next? What was it that was really bothering him? What was the root problem? These were a few of the thoughts that raced through my mind as I quickly prayed to know what I should say and do. "Why do you say that?" I asked. For the next several minutes he peppered me with issues—issues dealing with both doctrinal questions and historical events—that had been bothering him for some time. "Were you aware that Joseph Smith did such and such?" or "Were you aware that Brigham Young taught this or that?" or "How do you reconcile this with that?" Many of the issues and questions he raised were the typical things found in anti-Mormon literature or arguments from dissidents—so-called "Mormon intellectuals." I had encountered them many times before.

"Do you have a testimony?" I asked him point blank. "Have you ever felt the Holy Ghost testifying to you of the truthfulness of the restored gospel?"

"I am not sure anymore," he responded. "I think I once did."

We talked for a little while about what one must do to gain an unmistakable witness of the truth and how to recognize such a testimony. I explained to him how I had come to my testimony and how I have tried to answer or reconcile the tough questions he had raised. Despite this discussion, I could tell that the real issue was that his immoral conduct had caused him to lose the Spirit of the Lord, and he wasn't sure if he had the spiritual strength to get it back. "What if I do all the things you ask me to do and then I find out that the Church is not true?" he asked once again. "I'm not sure it's worth it." It seemed as if we had again hit a deadend in our discussion. Then a thought struck me like a thunderbolt.

"Where will you go? What will you do?" I asked him.

"What do you mean?" he responded with a look of bewilderment.

"Well, if you don't believe the Church is true and you don't want to live by its teachings, where are you now going to go with your life?" I asked again. "If you leave the Church and don't have any expectations to live gospel standards, how are you going to live your life? What will you do with your new freedom?"

"I don't know" was the only answer he could muster. He looked at me as if I had just kicked him in the stomach and knocked the wind out of him.

"Since you have such a problem with many of the teachings and practices of the Church and so many doubts concerning its truthfulness, you must have found something else—something better—that provides answers to all your questions and poses no difficult dilemmas for you," I stated. "Have you found something better?" I asked.

"No," was the answer—just as I had expected.

"Well then, it must be that life offers you more outside the Church," I responded. "If living the gospel makes you so miserable then you must find great happiness and fulfillment when you don't have to live by those standards. Is your life happier now?"

He sat there for a while looking at me, but in reality, he was staring past me. Pretty soon, tears welled up in his eyes and he stated, "No, my life isn't happier now. In fact, I hate my life. I am so unhappy when I do the things that I thought would bring me happiness." He paused for a moment and then said, "But what if the Church isn't true?" He left my office with the same question he had posed when he first entered.

I have thought much about this episode since it occurred. I wonder where this young man is today. I wonder how his life is progressing. As I think about him, I am reminded of an account in the scriptures where Jesus faced a somewhat similar scenario. From that event in Jesus' life comes a great lesson for all of us—a modern message couched within a setting in antiquity.

Just a day after five thousand men, plus women and children, were miraculously fed by the Savior with five barley loaves of bread and two small fish, Jesus delivered a powerful discourse that was controversial to say the least—even offensive to many. Despite the miracles that had been witnessed by so many, Jesus' "bread of life" discourse, given at the synagogue in Capernaum, caused many to shake their heads in disbelief. He declared that only through partaking of his flesh and blood could salvation and life eternal come to man. He was clearly teaching about the Atonement, but many did not understand the symbolism of his teachings or the doctrinal significance of what he was proclaiming. "This is an hard saying; who can hear it?" some of the disciples declared (John 6:60). I find it interesting that in several other translations of the New Testament, the reaction of the disciples is described in even stronger terms—"This is more than we can stomach! Why listen to such talk?"[1] "This is intolerable language! How could anyone accept it?"[2]

"Doth this offend you?" Jesus asked them upon seeing the mixed reactions to his doctrinal treatise on the Atonement and his definitive declaration of his messiahship. "There are some of you that believe not" (John 6:61, 64). Another translation has Jesus posing this question: "Does this make you want to give up?"[3] The teachings Jesus declared that day in the synagogue in Capernaum became a separation sermon, if you will. It became a separation of the true disciples, who could bear "hard sayings," from those who couldn't—a separation of those disciples who really desired to live the gospel from those who wanted only miracles and free food. "From that time many of his disciples went back, and walked no more with him" (John 6:66). Many no longer believed, despite all they had previously heard with their ears, witnessed with their eyes, and felt within their hearts. They no longer were disciples because they were troubled by and could not understand something the Master taught. "Will ye also go away?" Jesus asked the remaining disciples (John 6:67). His question is posed to each of us as well. Even today there are those who turn their backs on the Master and his anointed servants and his divine church because they are offended by someone or something and/or because they are spiritually troubled by certain teachings or practices they cannot fully comprehend. The circumstances and situations may change, but the issue remains the same: "Will ye also go away?" The implications of the Savior's question are as vitally important today as they were then.

In addition, Peter's faithful response is as much needed by modern disciples as it was by the ancients. "Lord, to whom shall we go? thou hast the words of eternal life" (John 6:68). These simple words—powerful beyond comprehension—provide us with needed direction when we personally, or those we love and serve, would turn back because they have been offended, deeply hurt, or because they have troubling doubts. This episode and Peter's words can help us deal with those critical moments when discipleship and endurance are put to the test. Sometimes those moments may be big things that, like a powerful earthquake, shake the very foundation of our souls. Often, however, they are little events that, like repeated tremors and aftershocks, cause gradual erosion of our testimonies.

Ultimately, this spiritual erosion, if unchecked, can compromise the foundation as much as one big earthquake. All of us will have moments when our discipleship and commitment to the kingdom are assaulted. That assault inevitably comes in a variety of ways—some blatantly in your face and others deviously disguised. What may be a "hard saying" or a difficult trial for one may not be so for another. We all get our feelings hurt at some time or another and it is all too easy to become offended whether such offense is intentional or innocent. Likewise, there will always be doctrines, teachings, practices, or historical events that we may not fully understand, agree with, or totally accept. There always has been and there always will be plenty around us in our sojourn in mortality to test our devotion and try our discipleship. How we deal with those times when we get our feelings hurt, how we react when our sensibilities are offended in some manner, and what we do to deal with those moments of vexing doubt or misunderstanding will make all the difference in the world (and beyond).

DEALING WITH OFFENSES AND HURT FEELINGS

Each of us is familiar with individuals who have been offended by someone or something in the Church and as a result have turned away from the gospel. "I will never go back to that Church as long as so and so is the bishop!" This statement, and many variations on the same theme, have been made by all too many people in all too many places and at all too many times. There probably isn't anyone in the Church—at least anyone who has reached the age of accountability and of somewhat normal mental capacity—who has not heard another say something or observed a person doing something that could be seen as offensive, insensitive, thoughtless, uncaring, or downright rude. Often these offenses are unintentional, but unfortunately there are those moments when the words and deeds are fully intended to offend, hurt, or alienate. Why would someone intentionally offend another? I can't answer that and I don't fully understand why but, unfortunately, I have seen it happen more often than it should, and I have witnessed the damaging effects.

The Church is comprised of mortal men and women with mortal weaknesses, "natural man" tendencies, diverse personalities, and character traits. Even those called to serve in leadership positions, though blessed with the mantle of the calling and gifts of the Spirit, do not leave behind all of their mortal foibles and frailties when they assume an office. The Church is not a country club for perfect people, but a place where imperfect people work together in the common cause of the gospel. We rub shoulders with many people from many different backgrounds. Sometimes we rub each other the wrong way, bump into one another, and step on each other's toes. Along the way our feelings can be left a little raw. I am convinced that one of the fundamental purposes of mortality is to learn to work with and appreciate people who may not always be easy to like, let alone love. Having Christlike love for all people doesn't happen spontaneously or automatically. It must be developed over time, like so many other traits of godliness. Since becoming more like God in our feelings for and our associations with all people is a fundamental purpose of earth life, we should not be surprised that service in the Church and associations with our fellowmen will be somewhat like a laboratory where the attributes of godliness we seek will be tested, tried, refined, and perfected. Dealing with hurt feelings, slights, injustices, insensitivities, rude comments, unfair judgments, and myriad other possible offenses is all part of that process of spiritual refinement. How we respond determines the depth and degree of our discipleship. Will we turn away like those who heard Jesus' words at Capernaum and were offended and "walked no more with him," or will we remain firm and steadfast like Peter?

I came to understand this challenge in a personal way. Many years ago our family moved into a new ward. Such transitions can be difficult. I think we were mentally prepared for the challenges of "homesickness," making new friends, and getting fully involved and immersed in a new church environment. I wasn't prepared, however, for some of the feelings I experienced in this new ward. We were virtually ignored for many weeks, and this we construed to be unfriendliness on the part of the ward members. No one went out of his way to speak to us and welcome us to the ward. We received no visits from home teachers, visiting teachers, or other ward leaders for many months. We desperately wanted to become involved, but no callings were forthcoming. Each week for several weeks my high priest group leader introduced me to the quorum as a visitor and asked me to introduce myself (as if he and they had never seen me before). It was a hard time, and I found myself struggling with feelings I had never felt before. Every Sunday became a trial to me. There was a very real temptation to "drop out" or find something else to do during church. "I'll show these people what they are missing," I fleetingly thought to myself. "We won't go to church and then they'll find out how much they need us." Because I was hurt or offended that they had not welcomed us into the ward and because of our not feeling needed, I was going to "punish" the ward for this slight.

Now, I can almost hear you say as you read this: "O, come on, Brother Top, get over it." Well, let me tell you—I said that to myself many times during those trying weeks. I knew that those feelings and thoughts were silly. Yet, there were times when I seriously thought that I would "punish" the ward for their unfriendliness and lack of fellowship. I was sure that by refusing to go to church the ward would suffer and would not be able to adequately function without us. "They'll come to see what a contribution we could have made to their ward." What a dumb thought! They didn't know we existed. How would our inactivity punish them? The ward had gone on quite well without us before we arrived (and they seemingly were doing quite well without our involvement). I quickly realized that they wouldn't even notice that they were being "punished" for their oversight of us. Who would I be punishing? It became abundantly clear that while I was nursing my hurt feelings, my family would be deprived of partaking of the sacrament and receiving gospel instruction. Worst of all, they would be deprived of seeing the example of a faithful father who was spiritually mature enough to deal with such a challenge. Who really would have been "punished" if I had selfishly acted upon my irrational thoughts resulting from my perceived slight and hurt feelings?

My own experience illustrates my point precisely. Sometimes we know in our heads how silly or illogical our thinking is, but we still feel hurt or offended and do, say, or think things that we wouldn't otherwise. It often begins with something simple or even silly. It may be something someone says. Even if it was not intended to be hurtful, it sometimes becomes even more offensive to us the longer we think about it, blow it out of proportion, and let our hurt feelings fester. That is one of Satan's tactics. He desires us to "make mountains out of molehills" and abandon rational thinking and act out of what we might call self-defense—getting back at those who offended us. Then he has us right where he wants us—cut off from the influence of the Holy Ghost, out of God's kingdom, and in Satan's domain and under his influence. Being easily offended is an attribute of the natural man—an attribute of self-centeredness and pride. Being easily offended is one of the first steps toward personal apostasy.

There is an example of this very thing from early Church history. It is the story of Thomas B. Marsh, president of the Quorum of the Twelve Apostles. His apostasy began over a trivial matter. He was offended by how his wife was treated by Church leaders and members after a disagreement concerning who should have the "strippings" of milk (cream). Taking offense and continuing to stew about how his family had been "mistreated" caused the small spiritual wound to fester until his soul was completely infected. Because he did not deal properly with the hurt feelings—his own and his wife's—his feelings of offense and anger at Church leaders grew larger and larger, ultimately ending in his apostasy and being cut off from the blessings of the gospel. What started as a very small matter—one that could have been easily resolved—ended in years and years of misery and family heartache.

In 1857, nearly twenty years after that critical moment, Brother Marsh decided he had harbored his hurt feelings long enough. He once again joined with the Saints and asked to be rebaptized. "I have not come here to seek for any office," he declared, "except it be to be a door-keeper or a deacon; no, I am neither worthy nor fit; but I want a place among you as a humble servant of the Lord."[4] It had been a painful lesson to learn, but Thomas B. Marsh learned that whatever had caused his hurt feelings, whatever had been the source of his offense, was not worth the misery that came when he turned back and "walked no more" with the Saints. His words to the Saints gathered on Temple Square in the old Bowery in September 1857 serve as a valuable warning to any today who may be offended at times and then be tempted to turn back, get even, or stay away:

"If there are any among this people who should ever apostatize and do as I have done, prepare your backs for a good whipping, if you are such as the Lord loves. But if you will take my advice, you will stand by the authorities; but if you go away and the Lord loves you as much as he did me, he will whip you back again.

"Many have said to me, 'How is it that a man like you, who understood so much of the revelations of God as recorded in the Book of Doctrine and Covenants, should fall away?' I told them not to feel too secure, . . . for before you think of it, your steps will slide. You will not then think nor feel for a moment as you did before you lost the Spirit of Christ; for when men [become offended and] apostatize, they are left to grovel in the dark. . . .

" . . . Let me tell you, my brethren and friends, if you do not want to suffer in body and mind, as I have done,—if there are any of you that have the seeds of apostasy in you, do not let them make their appearance, but nip that spirit in the bud; for it is misery and affliction in this world, and destruction in the world to come."[5]

Each of us could be offended and nurse hurt feelings every moment of our lives. Whether it be at home, at work, at church, or on the golf course, we could take offense at virtually everything and anything someone says or does to us. We could spend every waking moment (and in our dreams when we sleep) rehashing events in which we were slighted. We could (and unfortunately some do) read ill will and malice into all that another says or does. What a waste of time, intellectual and emotional energy, spirituality, and personal peace! This waste becomes especially apparent when we realize that almost all things that *could have* offended us were never intended to do so. Another's actions may have been thoughtless and insensitive, but not mean or malicious. I certainly hope that those I deal with give me that benefit of the doubt when I say or do something that could be construed as offensive or insensitive. I certainly never intend to hurt feelings. I would feel terrible if I did. So would others. Why can't we extend the same consideration to others that we would want for ourselves?

Unfortunately, there *are* times when a person may have legitimate justification for being offended, hurt, embarrassed, or humiliated in some way. Thoughtless, uncaring, and insensitive things are done and said every day. Even when we are justified in taking offense, how we react speaks volumes about our personal character and discipleship—who we really are, what we really believe, and who we are seeking to follow. Several years ago, Elder John H. Groberg of the Seventy told a story in general conference that beautifully illustrates this principle.

"In the early 1900s, a young father and his family joined the Church in Hawaii. He was enthused about his new-found religion, and after two years of membership both he and his eldest son held the priesthood. They prospered and enjoyed the fellowship of the little branch. They anxiously looked forward to being sealed as a family for eternity in the temple soon to be completed in Laie.

"Then, as so often happens, a test crossed their path. One of their daughters became ill with an unknown disease and was taken away to a strange hospital. People in Hawaii were understandably wary of unknown diseases, as such diseases had wrought so much havoc there.

"The concerned family went to church the next Sunday, looking forward to the strength and understanding they would receive from their fellow members. It was a small branch. This young father and his son very often took the responsibility for blessing and passing the sacrament. This was one such Sunday. They reverently broke the bread while the congregation sang the sacrament hymn. When the hymn was finished, the young father began to kneel to offer the sacrament prayer. Suddenly the branch president, realizing who was at the sacred table, sprang to his feet. He pointed his finger and cried, 'Stop. You can't touch the sacrament. Your daughter has an unknown disease. Leave immediately while someone else fixes new sacrament bread. We can't have you here. Go.'

"How would you react? What would you do?

"The stunned father slowly stood up. He searchingly looked at the branch president, then at the congregation. Then, sensing the depth of anxiety and embarrassment from all, he motioned to his family and they quietly filed out of the chapel.

"Not a word was said as, with faces to the ground, they moved along the dusty trail to their small home. The young son noticed the firmness in his father's clenched fists and the tenseness of his set jaw. When they entered their home they all sat in a circle, and the father said, 'We will be silent until I am ready to speak.' All sorts of thoughts went through the mind of this young boy. He envisioned his father coming up with many novel ways of getting revenge. Would they kill the branch president's pigs, or burn his house, or join another church? He could hardly wait to see what would happen.

"Five minutes, ten minutes, fifteen minutes—not a sound. He glanced at his father. His eyes were closed, his mouth was set, his fingers clenched, but no sound. Twenty minutes, twenty-five minutes—still nothing. Then he noticed a slight relaxing of his father's hands, a small tremor on his father's lips, then a barely perceptible sob. He looked at his father—tears were trickling down his cheeks from closed eyes. Soon he noticed his mother was crying also, then one child, then another, and soon the whole family.

"Finally, the father opened his eyes, cleared his throat, and announced, 'I am now ready to speak. Listen carefully.' He slowly turned to his wife and said, meaningfully, 'I love you.' Then turning to each child, he told them individually, 'I love you. I love all of you and I want us to be together, forever, as a family. And the only way that can be is for all of us to be good members of The Church of Jesus Christ of Latter-day Saints, and be sealed by his holy priesthood in the temple. This is not the branch president's church. It is the Church of Jesus Christ. We will not let any man or any amount of hurt or embarrassment or pride keep us from being together forever. Next Sunday we will go back to church. We will stay by ourselves until our daughter's sickness is known, but we will go back.'

"This great man had proper eternal perspective.

"The daughter's health problem was resolved; the family did go to the temple when it was completed. The children did remain faithful and were likewise sealed to their own families in the temple as time went on. Today over 100 souls in this family are active members of the Church and call their father, grandfather, and great-grandfather blessed because he kept his eyes on eternity."[6]

Dealing with Doubts and Questions

In addition to hurt feelings, there is another form of offense that often causes would-be disciples to turn back and "walk no more with him." That is doubt about the divinity of the Restoration and vexing questions concerning doctrine. Jesus' disciples were troubled by what they called "hard sayings" when they could not understand or accept what Jesus taught. Even today there are those who become offended, turn their back on the gospel, and leave the Church over doctrinal and historical issues they cannot accept or other kinds of questions they cannot adequately resolve. "Will ye also go away?" remains a relevant question for these individuals as well.

Through the years I have encountered many people, young and old, in my classes at BYU and through my various ecclesiastical assignments who were on the verge of leaving the Church over such concerns and doubts. One student was experiencing a crisis of faith because there was no archaeological evidence to support the story of the flood in Noah's time. Likewise, he wasn't sure he could believe the historicity of the scriptures because there was no historical corroboration of the Egyptian plagues in Moses' day or the miraculous crossing of the Red Sea. One ward member refused to come to church or go to the temple because women couldn't hold the priesthood. "Did Joseph Smith really practice plural marriage?" is a question that has been posed to me hundreds of times. "Why did we practice polygamy at all?" One student boldly announced, "I cannot believe in a God who plays favorites and has a chosen people." "What about the Mountain Meadows massacre?" "Why couldn't blacks have the priesthood before 1978?" I could go on and on with similar questions and doctrinal concerns I have heard from others through the years.

Whatever the issue or concern, for that individual the topic is a "hard saying"—just like the Master's teachings on the Bread of Life. These concerns can become critical crossroads for someone who has doubts or seemingly irreconcilable issues. How we deal with these issues is just as vital to faithful discipleship as is dealing with hurt feelings. Although they may be different in some ways, dealing with both kinds of offenses requires an eternal perspective, a willingness to see beyond intellectual responses alone and see with spiritual eyes and hear the voice of the Spirit. Both require faith and a lot of patience.

Sometimes there is no adequate answer or explanation that can dispel all doubt and resolve all questions and concerns. What, then, can we do? Instead of throwing in the towel, so to speak, and turning your back on the Lord and his gospel, there are some things that can be done. These suggestions may not satisfy everyone, but I know they work. They have helped me at critical times in my life and I have seen them bless the lives of others. They may seem simplistic to some, but I can't help that. Sometimes the simpler the suggestion, the more significant the result. These helps, if used when needed, can be like anchors to the soul when one is in troubled waters or a life preserver to one who is desperately seeking to keep his head above water to avoid drowning in a sea of doubt.

1. Be willing to withhold judgment and put some things on the shelf. There is a tendency for us to want our answers and concerns resolved immediately, if not sooner. For many doctrinal matters, that isn't possible because the Lord has not yet seen fit to reveal all things. There is one example I encounter every semester in my classes. That is seeking to understand and reconcile organic evolution with the doctrine of the Creation and the Fall. I would love to be able to know all things and reconcile all seeming contradictions, but I can't right now. So I have to be willing to say, "I don't know" and wait patiently until the Lord sees fit to finally clear up the picture. To do this isn't a cop-out, nor need it shake our faith. "We believe all that God has revealed, all that He does now reveal, and we believe that He will yet reveal many great and important things pertaining to the Kingdom of God" (Article of Faith 9).

Elder Bruce R. McConkie gave some insightful counsel concerning this matter in a general letter addressed to "Honest Truth Seekers." He explained: "To those with full insight and complete understanding there are no hard questions. After a mystery has been solved it is no longer a mystery. But there are some questions which seem to invite intellectual forays into unknown areas, or which seem to ensnare, in endless contention, those who are somewhat less than spiritually literate.

"If you cannot believe all of the doctrines of the gospel, withhold judgment in the areas in question. Do not commit yourself to a position which is contrary to that espoused by the prophets and Apostles who preside over the kingdom. Study, pray, work in the Church and await further light and knowledge.

"If you are troubled about [anything that has not been fully revealed or adequately taught and explained by the prophets of God] withhold judgment and do not take a stand against the scriptures. . . .

". . . Do not commit yourself to the defense of a false cause. Study something else and await the day when you will be prepared for more light on the matter that troubles you."[7]

2. Maintain an eternal perspective—look at the big picture. Several years ago Elder Richard G. Scott used an object lesson in one of his general conference talks that certainly has many applications. It applies well to this specific suggestion. He spoke of the remarkable beauty of the earth and the magnificent opportunities of life. He said, "A pebble held close to the eye appears to be a gigantic obstacle. Cast on the ground, it is seen in perspective."[8] A doctrinal doubt or unresolved issue can be like that pebble that blocks the view of everything else—all that is "virtuous, lovely, or of good report or praiseworthy" in the gospel. That pebble of doubt, though it may be troubling and important, cannot become a boulder—a spiritual eclipse that blocks out all light and enlightenment. It has to be put down on the ground, so to speak, and viewed in proper perspective—an eternal perspective. "There is so much to learn about the great eternal verities which shape our destiny," Elder McConkie observed, "that it seems a shame to turn our attention everlastingly to the minutiae and insignificant things.

"So often questions like this are asked: 'I know it is not essential to my salvation, but I would really like to know how many angels can dance on the head of a pin and if it makes any difference whether the pin is made of brass or bronze?' There is such a thing as getting so tied up with the little fly specks on the great canvas which depicts the whole plan of salvation that we lose sight of what the life and the light and the glory of eternal reward are all about. . . . There is such a thing as virtually useless knowledge, the acquisition of which won't make one iota of difference to the destiny of the kingdom or the salvation of its subjects."[9]

If I am struggling with a doctrinal issue, I need to look at the big picture—the whole plan of salvation—rather than just focusing on one little brushstroke on the canvas of the gospel. If I am troubled by an event in church history, I need to look at and appreciate the entire panoramic, epic story of the Restoration, not just the "outtakes." We will never see things as they really are if we focus our gaze only on warts and slight blemishes—never examining the straight teeth, the fair complexion, the striking features, the beautiful hair, and all the other remarkable features, including an inner beauty the eye can't see. I will never have an eternal perspective and as a result will never find the answers or resolution I seek, if I hold the pebble—whatever doubt or unresolved issue that pebble may be—in front of my eyes, blocking my view of all else.

3. Not all sources are of equal worth—give the Lord "equal time." It is important for us to remember that having questions, unresolved issues, and even doubts is not necessarily evil. The real challenge is what we do with them. "Doubt is not wrong unless it becomes an end of life. It rises to high dignity when it becomes an active search for, and practice of, truth," wrote Elder John A. Widtsoe. "Doubt which immediately leads to honest inquiry, and thereby removes itself, is wholesome. But that doubt which feeds and grows upon itself, and, with stubborn indolence, breeds more doubt, is evil."[10]

My experience through years dealing with students and others who have come to a crisis of their faith because of doubts, unanswered questions, and unresolved issues has taught me that not all sources are of equal worth. Usually, one who has come to such a crossroad and is tempted to leave the Church has spent more time and effort searching in some sources—often questionable sources by their very nature—than the more reliable sources. Just as a journalist must obtain verifiable information from the most reliable sources for the news story to be factual and trustworthy, so too must we in our spiritual quest for truth. Some sources are better than others. There are secondary sources and primary sources even in spiritual inquiry. Each can provide important information. Secondary sources are secondhand—the opinions, feelings, experiences, and teachings of someone else. They are not bad sources of information, but they are not the most important or reliable. The primary sources are the scriptures and the teachings of the prophets and apostles—especially those living in our days and speaking directly to us. You will never get the spiritual truth you desperately seek—you will never have your doubts dispelled and answerable questions adequately resolved—unless you search and rely on these primary sources more than secondary ones, whatever those may be. If the Lord or his prophets can answer our questions, why would we then go to cynics and critics—those whose objective is to muddy the waters and destroy faith—for our information? Elder M. Russell Ballard of the Quorum of the Twelve taught this principle with the following personal story:

"One of my missionaries came to me some time ago. He was a fine missionary. I asked him, 'Elder, how can I help you?'

"'President,' he said, 'I think I'm losing my testimony.'

"I couldn't believe it. I asked him how that could be possible.

"'For the first time I have read some anti-Mormon literature,' he said. 'I have some questions, and nobody will answer them for me. I am confused, and I think I am losing my testimony.'

"I asked him what his questions were, and he told me. They were the standard anti-Church issues, but I wanted a little time to gather materials so I could provide meaningful answers. So we set up an appointment ten days later, at which time I told him I would answer every one of his questions. As he started to leave, I stopped him.

"'Elder, you've asked me several questions here today,' I said. 'Now I have one for you.'

" 'Yes, President.'

" 'How long has it been since you read from the Book of Mormon?' I asked.

"His eyes dropped. He looked at the floor for a while. Then he looked at me. 'It's been a long time, President,' he confessed.

" 'All right,' I said. 'You have given me my assignment. It's only fair that I give you yours. I want you to promise me that you will read in the Book of Mormon for at least one hour every day between now and our next appointment.' He agreed that he would do that.

"Ten days later he returned to my office, and I was ready. I pulled out my papers to start answering his questions. But he stopped me.

" 'President,' he said, 'that isn't going to be necessary.' Then he explained, 'I know the Book of Mormon is true. I know Joseph Smith is a prophet of God.'

" 'Well, that's great,' I said, 'but you're going to get answers to your questions anyway. I worked a long time on this, so you just sit there and listen.'

"And so I answered all of those questions, and then asked, 'Elder, what have you learned from this?'

"And he said, 'Give the Lord equal time.' "[11]

4. Don't throw the baby out with the bath water! Unfortunately, there is an almost universal human tendency to think the whole is bad if one part is defective. Yet, we all realize how silly it would be to assume that an expensive car has gone bad and needs to be junked when only a small fuse is blown. There are those that do the same thing with regard to the Church and the gospel. If there is something—usually something fairly small and unimportant—that causes concern, doubt, or problems in some way, they call everything into question. For example, if one has a problem with Book of Mormon geography—whether there were one or two Cumorahs, whether there is any archaeological evidence for Hebrew or reformed Egyptian in the New World, or any other similar question about the Book of Mormon—it would seem awfully silly to then totally and absolutely dismiss the divinity of that book. There are numerous examples of how some do this—they no longer have use for the bath water so they get rid of the baby too.

I heard an interesting perspective on this from an unexpected source a while back as I listened to the radio. My ears perked up and my interest was piqued when I heard a Latter-day Saint woman call in to the Dr. Laura Schlessinger radio show. She told Dr. Laura that she was thinking about leaving the Church because she couldn't believe such things as the First Vision, visitation of angels, gold plates, and modern revelation. The woman had been on a mission, married in the temple, was active in the Church, and a wife and mother in what she characterized as a "model Mormon family." Yet her questions and doubts were consuming her.

Dr. Laura wasn't very sympathetic and reminded the caller of things in Judaism, Christianity, and other religions that some would have similar doubts about. "Why would you have a problem with those things," Dr. Laura asked, "but not with things like a burning bush, angels, changing water to wine, walking on water, raising the dead? All religions have things that are hard to believe. That is what faith is all about!"

With that strong statement, the Latter-day Saint caller realized the incongruity of her doubts, but she still maintained that she wasn't sure she could believe in Mormonism any longer. Dr. Laura then took an approach I found very insightful and helpful. "What if everybody was a Mormon?" Dr. Laura asked. "Would the world be a better place or a worse place as a result? Is your family better off or worse off because of your beliefs? Is your life better or worse because of the Church?"

Somewhat taken aback by these questions, the woman had to admit that the world would be a better place if everyone lived the principles espoused by the Church. She admitted that her family was stronger and better as well because of gospel teachings.

"Well, then, why would you be willing to get rid of all that?" Dr. Laura asked. "Isn't that rather selfish and shortsighted—that you would be willing to throw away all that is good, including your family—because you have a few doubts or unresolved issues?" I was impressed with that declaration. I couldn't have said it better myself.

5. Remember the spiritual witnesses and feelings you have had in the past. Perhaps the most important of all suggestions—in fact, the only one that in the end really matters—is never to forget the testimony that you have previously received and the spiritual feelings and guidance you have experienced in your life. There will always be tests and trials of faith and testimony. Opposition is an integral part of the plan. Why, then, should we be surprised when we have experiences or questions that pose a challenge in some way to our testimonies, as well as to our devotion and commitment? In fact, we can expect Satan to test our testimonies and try our faith. He did with Moses, Nephi, Alma, Jesus, Joseph Smith, and many others of great spiritual stature. What can we do when we face such an assault? I believe that one of the most important things you and I can do is to remember—to recall in specific detail what we learned and how we felt—when the Lord did bear witness of truth to us previously. Even when I have questions and feel like I don't have good answers, I can remember and cling to that spiritual witness. When an angel asked Nephi, "Knowest thou the condescension of God?" he responded: "*I know* that he loveth his children; *nevertheless, I do not know the meaning of all things*" (1 Nephi 11:16–17; emphasis added). Nephi didn't have all the answers, but what he did know was his rock-solid foundation. It is the same for us today. *What we know* by the power of the Holy Ghost is far more important than *what we don't know* and what we cannot fully understand with our mortal intellect alone.

There is an important and comforting verse in the Doctrine and Covenants that can serve to strengthen us when Satan seeks to cloud our minds and challenge our convictions. To Oliver Cowdery, who had his own questions about Joseph Smith's prophetic mantle and who sought a further witness concerning the truthfulness of the Restoration, the Lord declared: "Verily, verily, I say unto you, if you desire a further witness, cast your mind upon the night that you cried unto me in your heart, that you might know concerning the truth of these things.

"Did I not speak peace to your mind concerning the matter? What greater witness can you have than from God?

"And now, behold, you have received a witness; for if I have told you things which no man knoweth have you not received a witness?" (D&C 6:22–24).

If, and when, moments of doubt about this issue or that tempt us to be offended at "hard sayings" and tempt us to "walk no more with him," we can do as Oliver Cowdery was admonished, and cast our minds back upon those times when we felt the Spirit and *knew* with all our heart. As we do this we will be able to say, like Jacob when challenged by Sherem, the anti-Christ, "I had heard the voice of the Lord . . . wherefore, I could not be shaken" (Jacob 7:5). I was deeply impressed, moved, and comforted by the counsel and promise given by Elder Jeffrey R. Holland to students at Brigham Young University. I believe his words have relevance and application to all of us—whatever our age, circumstance, or individualized test:

"Of course our faith will be tested as we fight through these self-doubts and second thoughts. Some days we will be miraculously led out of Egypt—seemingly free, seemingly on our way—only to come to yet another confrontation, like all that water lying before us. *At those times we must resist the temptation to panic and to give up.* At those times fear will be the strongest of the adversary's weapons against us. . . .

". . . After you have gotten the message, after you have paid the price to feel his love and hear the word of the Lord, 'go forward.' Don't fear, don't vacillate, don't quibble, don't whine. . . . With the spirit of revelation, dismiss your fears and wade in with both feet. . . .

"Fighting through darkness and despair and pleading for the light is what opened this dispensation. It is what keeps it going, and it is what will keep you going."[12]

"TO WHOM SHALL WE GO? THOU HAST THE WORDS OF ETERNAL LIFE"

A few years ago, one of my colleagues in Religious Education at BYU reported on his visit to a symposium that discussed the Church and its doctrines, history, culture, and so on. Participants in the symposium and the members of the sponsoring organization included some members of the Church who would consider themselves mainstream, and others who were critics of the Church—some dissident members with issues concerning Church doctrines or practices, some nonmembers who are highly critical of the Church, and some curious yet misguided members who, like the ancient Athenians, desired "to hear some new thing" (Acts 17:21). My colleague reported that at one of the sessions the presenter spent most of the hour talking about all the idiosyncrasies of "Mormon culture." The audience roared with laughter at the humorous anecdotes. In many respects the descriptions were designed to make the Church look provincial, backwards, narrow-minded, out of touch, even silly. "How could any serious-minded person affiliate with and believe in the doctrines of a Church like this?" was the underlying current. It appeared that the whole purpose of the presentation was to mock and belittle the Church. However, that all changed quickly and dramatically as the presenter delivered his concluding statement. "We can laugh at all these things," he said, "but don't discount or dismiss the Church and its teachings." The room became very quiet and the mood was suddenly very serious. "I have been out in the world. I have seen what is out there," he continued. "You may have issues or problems with the Church, but let me tell you, it's still the best thing out there." With that he sat down and many in the audience were stunned. That certainly was not what they wanted or expected to hear.

Of course, there are going to be times when we get our toes stepped on or our feelings hurt as we sojourn through mortality. We shouldn't be surprised by it. It is an integral part of the test. As we travel through life in God's earthly vehicle—The Church of Jesus Christ of Latter-day Saints—we may feel crowded and squeezed at times, maybe even elbowed a time or two, but we must not get off the bus. It is the only one going where we want to go. As we journey we may look out the window and think the grass is greener elsewhere. But, as I have heard my friend and colleague Robert L. Millet say, "The reason it looks greener is that it's artificial turf—it's not even the real thing." We would be sadly disappointed to get off the bus to frolic in the green fields of the world only to discover that what we thought we desired was nothing more than Astroturf®—an imitation of the real thing.

There may be hurt feelings along the way. In most cases, the slights and insensitivities we encounter will be unintentional. There will be times, however, where the offenses against us may be egregious, but we must not abandon the ship. To do so—whether it be because of hurt feelings or unresolved questions or doubts—is like going on a cruise ship and jumping overboard if the waiter is rude or the meal is not what we wanted. If the flight attendant spills tomato juice on me, if the person next to me snores, or if I don't like the in-flight movie, I'm still not going to jump out of the airplane.

"Will ye also go away?" the Savior asked the disciples when others were turning their backs on Jesus and his gospel. "To whom shall we go?" Peter asked. "Thou hast the words of eternal life." Truly, there is nowhere else to go. He is the way—the only way. "Neither is there salvation in any other: for there is none other name under heaven given among men, whereby we must be saved" (Acts 4:12; see also 2 Nephi 25:20; Mosiah 3:17; 4:7–8).

Notes

1. John 6:60, *New English Bible*.

2. John 6:30, *Jerusalem Bible*.

3. John 6:61, *Today's English Version*.

4. Thomas Marsh, in *Journal of Discourses*, 26 vols. (London: Latter-day Saints' Book Depot, 1854–86), 5:208.

5. Ibid., 5:206–7.

6. John H. Groberg, in Conference Report, April 1980, 69–70.

7. Bruce R. McConkie, in *Doctrines of the Restoration: Sermons and Writings of Bruce R. McConkie*, ed. Mark L. McConkie (Salt Lake City: Bookcraft, 1989), 232–33.

8. Richard G. Scott, in Conference Report, April 1996, 32.

9. McConkie, *Doctrines of the Restoration*, 232.

10. John A. Widtsoe, *Evidences and Reconciliations* (Salt Lake City: Bookcraft, 1987), 32–33.

11. M. Russell Ballard, "When Shall These Things Be?" in *Brigham Young University 1995–96 Speeches* (Provo, Utah: Brigham Young University, 1996), 191–92.

12. Jeffrey R. Holland, "Cast Not Away Therefore Your Confidence," *Brigham Young University 1998–99 Speeches* (Provo, Utah: Brigham Young University, 1999), 159–60.

CHAPTER 9

THE LIGHT OF LIFE

I love to garden. I find it both therapeutic and instructional. Working the soil, planting flowers and vegetables, pruning, watering, and weeding are not only good for my body but also my mind and soul. Often as I work in my yard and garden, I receive instruction as I observe God's handiwork in nature or open my heart to promptings from the Spirit that seem to come more clearly when I am away from the hectic pace and noises of everyday life. Great lessons—gospel lessons and lessons of life— can be learned in the garden. One lesson I have learned has to do with light. It is fascinating to watch seeds germinate in the soil and grow and reach toward the sunlight. There are plants and flowers that exert enormous effort to obtain all the light they need— sometimes even turning and stretching toward the sun. Without light they could not live, thrive, or produce their fruit and flowers. In a very literal sense, light "giveth life to all things" (D&C 88:13).

People, like plants, also need light to survive and thrive. Light deprivation can have serious side effects, both physically and emotionally. Although I have never suffered any serious light deprivation, I have had several experiences with darkness that have profoundly taught me the importance of light, both physical and spiritual.

When we lived in the Holy Land one of my favorite places to take my family and my students from the BYU Jerusalem Center was "Micah's cave" (named because of its location near the hometown of the Old Testament prophet Micah; it was also sometimes referred to by the locals as the "Mormon cave" because so many students from the "Mormon University" went there). Not only was it fun to explore the nooks and crannies of the labyrinth of connecting caves, but there was a spiritual lesson that could be drawn from our explorations. To get into Micah's cave, we had to crawl on hands and knees, wiggling and squirming like inchworms through some tight places with challenging twists and turns. The cave is not a place for large or long people or those who suffer from claustrophobia. One by one we would crawl through the rock tunnel until we all were gathered in a larger room or cavern located at the end of the tunnel. It was pitch-black dark and stuffy from lack of ventilation. With all of our flashlights turned off, we could actually feel the darkness. We could hear others breathing around us, but could not see them. We felt trapped and closed in on all sides by an oppressive darkness.

In this setting, we sang hymns about light, such as "The Lord Is My Light," "Lead, Kindly Light," and "Teach Me to Walk in the Light." We read scriptures about light versus darkness. "I am the light of the world," the Savior taught (John 8:12). "In him was life; and the life was the light of men," John testified of Jesus. "And the light shineth in darkness; and the darkness comprehended it not" (John 1:4–5). In this dark and stuffy setting, these verses took on new meaning—especially when we finally ascended out of the dark depths of the cave into sunshine and fresh air. The oppressive darkness was swallowed up by the light of day. The claustrophobic feelings of captivity were dispelled by the true liberation that accompanies light and life.

In contrast to those of us who were vividly aware of the darkness and constriction in Micah's cave, there are those around us who, in a spiritual sense, are "walking in darkness at noon-day" (D&C 95:6). They are alive, yet lack life. They see light, but lack enlightenment. They see the world, but are blind to the things of God. Even in the Church, there are some who walk by dim flashlights with batteries nearly depleted, as it were, when a powerful floodlight—the Light of the World—is fully charged and always at their disposal. There are those who are ignorantly content to live in a cave when a whole world of breathtaking beauty and infinite possibilities awaits them above. There are those who live, yet lack life—the Abundant Life. To these, and to all of us, the Savior offers life and light—a Light and Life far beyond mere sight and sustenance.

LIGHT AND LIFE: SYMBOLS OF ETERNAL GLORY

There are specific episodes in the life of the Master—miracles performed by the Son of God—that illustrate this and serve as a doctrinal backdrop to his invitation to us today to partake of Light and Life. One miracle dealt with a man who was blind from birth and received a restoration from darkness to light. Another records the raising of a dead man from his sepulchre of four days—a restoration from death to life. Each was a beneficiary of the Master's healing touch. Each miracle also conveyed a message, one intended not only for those who observed these miraculous healings but also a message for us today.

As Jesus walked out of the gates to the temple complex in Jerusalem, a man blind since birth sat on the steps with hands outstretched for alms. "Master, who did sin," the disciples asked, "this man, or his parents, that he was born blind?" (John 9:2). Jesus explained that the man's blindness was not a result of sin on the part of either the parents or the man himself. Rather, this man's blindness was to be the means by which "the works of God should be made manifest" in Christ (vs. 3).

"I must work the works of him that sent me, while it is day: the night cometh, when no man can work.

"As long as I am in the world, I am the light of the world.

"When he had thus spoken, he spat on the ground, and made

clay of the spittle, and he anointed the eyes of the blind man with the clay,

"And said unto him, Go, wash in the pool of Siloam, (which is by interpretation, Sent.) He went his way therefore, and washed, and came seeing" (John 9:4–7).

Many of the blind man's acquaintances rejoiced at this remarkable healing, but when the Pharisees heard of it, they sought to kill Jesus for breaking the Sabbath day. When the healed man testified before the council of Pharisees that Jesus had indeed restored his sight by the power of God, he was ridiculed and reviled, called a sinner, and ultimately cast out of the synagogue because of his testimony of Christ and the miracles He performed.

"Jesus heard that they had cast him out; and when he had found him, he said unto him, Dost thou believe on the Son of God?

"He answered and said, Who is he, Lord, that I might believe on him?

"And Jesus said unto him, Thou hast both seen him, and it is he that talketh with thee.

"And he said, Lord, I believe. And he worshipped him" (John 9:35–38).

Not only do the Master's miracles temporally bless the recipient—by healing the sick, cleansing the leper, making the lame to walk, the blind to see, and the deaf to hear—but they also heal spiritually too, strengthening the faith of recipient and observers alike and testify of the divinity of the Son of God. In addition to this, each miracle that blesses an individual typifies the ultimate miracle of the Atonement, which blesses all mankind. In this case, an individual who had lived his entire life in the darkness of physical blindness was now able to see and to have his life filled with light, color, and images. He was able to see the faces of people he loved, and who loved him. But more important, he was able to see the Light of the World and come to know him. Giving sight to the blind, though a physical miracle, testified to all who witnessed or heard of it that through the atonement of Jesus Christ the "scales of [spiritual] darkness" will be lifted as every knee bows and every tongue confesses that Jesus is the Christ. All will be brought out of the darkness of mortality into the light of immortality. All will stand in the presence of God to be judged. Like the healed blind man, we too will have opportunity to gaze upon the light-filled face of the Son of God. We will see the Light of the World and behold his glory. Those who have come to truly know the Master, have partaken of his atoning sacrifice, have kept his commandments, and have submitted to the ordinances of the gospel will likewise be filled with light and glory that surpasses all understanding. These will not only see the Light, but be in the Light, and become like the Light. They will have eternal life—eternal light.

Outside the tomb of his beloved friend Lazarus, who had died only a few days earlier, Jesus declared: "I am the resurrection, and the life: he that believeth in me, though he were dead, yet shall he live" (John 11:25). On at least two other occasions the Lord had raised the dead, but the miraculous raising of Lazarus was even more remarkable. Lazarus had been dead four days—significant to the Jews because they believed that after three days the spirit could not reenter the body. To the Jews, death became final at that point. Decomposition had already begun its gruesome work. While Mary and Martha perhaps feared that even Jesus could not now revive Lazarus and while others mocked the prospects of raising one from the dead at any time—let alone after four days—Jesus stepped forward "that the Son of God might be glorified thereby" (John 11:4). With the spoken word, "Lazarus, come forth," a mighty miracle was performed. "And he that was dead came forth" (John 11:43–44).

This astonishing miracle truly testified of Christ's life-giving powers, but even more, it foreshadowed a greater miracle—the resurrection of the Life of the World. Through Jesus' death and resurrection, we too will be possessors of life—immortality. Because his tomb is empty, so will ours be someday. As the apostle John declared: "God hath given to us eternal life, and this life is in his Son. He that hath the Son hath life" (1 John 5:11–12).

THE ABUNDANT LIFE

As the Light and Life of the world, Jesus offers all of us light and life—not only in the eternal worlds, but here in mortality as well. "I am come that they might have life," he declared, "and that they might have it more abundantly" (John 10:10). His message of life and light was not merely for the next life, but also to give guidance, purpose, and joy in this life. His miracles were not only types and shadows of the ultimate miracle of his atonement, but also acts of compassion intended to make mortal life better—filled with more goodness and happiness and less pain and hopelessness. The light and life he extends to us is not just reserved in waiting for some far-off day in a far-off realm, but for right here and right now.

You have probably heard the slang phrases such as, "Get a life!" or "He has no life." Clearly these phrases do not refer to the physiological definition of life—breathing, a beating heart, and a functioning brain. They refer to someone who has physiological life but lacks something deeper, more qualitative. There is an episode from the life of the Savior that illustrates this. It shows that he, as the Light of Life, can not only restore life to the dead, but give life to the living.

"And, behold, a woman, which was diseased with an issue of blood twelve years, came behind him, and touched the hem of his garment:

"For she said within herself, If I may but touch his garment, I shall be whole.

"But Jesus turned him about, and when he saw her, he said,

Daughter, be of good comfort; thy faith hath made thee whole. And the woman was made whole from that hour" (Matthew 9:20–22).

Many Bible scholars believe that the "issue of blood" was a gynecological condition called menorrhagia, which caused her to have a continual flow of menstrual blood. Under Levitical law, this would make her perpetually "unclean" (see Leviticus 15). In this condition she would not be allowed to move freely among the people; anyone she touched would thus become unclean as well. She would be somewhat ostracized from society at large. Because of this chronic condition, this woman—this daughter of Zion—would be unable to marry or have children.[1] She would not have been able to realize her highest hopes for posterity, as was and is the hope of all faithful sons and daughters of Father Abraham. She had life. She could walk and talk and eat and see, but she lacked the kind of life that she most earnestly desired.

She could not touch Jesus or ask him to lay his hands on her head and heal her, for so doing would make him unclean under the law. Her only chance for healing would be a simple touch of the "hem of the garment"—a border that symbolized all the blessings of the Abrahamic covenant. She could do nothing else but pray. "Daughter," Jesus said to her, no doubt referring to her role as a daughter of Abraham, with a desire to be not only a daughter but also a mother in Zion, "Be of good comfort; thy faith hath made thee whole." Cured from her disease, this woman could now be clean. Being clean she could have her desires realized. She had been alive previously, but through the love, compassion, and healing touch of the Master, she could now be whole—she could have a life, an abundant life. Healed by the hand of the Lord and cleansed from her perpetual uncleanness, this faithful daughter of Abraham was able to experience a new life and then become a giver of life in her own right.

I have always loved this story, for it represents something much more expansive than an isolated healing of one individual. To me, the woman with an "issue of blood" represents all mankind in a way. All of us may have breath, relatively good health, enough to eat, maybe even a nice house and a good job, but lack the abundant life—the fulfillment of all of our spiritual yearnings. Just as the Savior gave her "newness of life" and a quality of life that she could not have realized otherwise, he offers us the same. We too can be filled with the "light of life." His gospel can give us light and direction in a darkened world. It teaches us how to live in ways that will bring happiness and fulfillment. It teaches us that we must love others as he loves us. This gives light and life to our own lives, enriches our relationships with others, and fills our hearts with God's love. That is the kind of life he desires us to possess in abundance.

LIGHT AND LIFE: FORGIVENESS OF SINS AND THE COMPANIONSHIP OF THE HOLY GHOST

Jesus gives the world *life* through the promise of a universal resurrection and *light* through overcoming the effects of spiritual death, which came upon all men through the Fall. Each of us will receive some level of light as we return to the Father's presence for judgment and inherit a glory of eternal reward. To people of the world who abide by the teachings of the Master comes *general* improvement in the quality of life and enlightenment. To those who then commit themselves fully to him and his gospel come *specific* promises of light and life. The gospel of Jesus Christ is more than a set of ethical principles or practical suggestions for daily living. Although those who view Jesus' life and teachings in this manner will be blessed with a degree of light and life, there is, however, much, much more light and life at stake. The Savior has promised this to those who are his true disciples. "I am the light of the world: he that *followeth me* shall not walk in darkness, but shall have the light of life" (John 8:12; emphasis added). The key phrase in this verse is "followeth me." It connotes more than verbal assent or even a general adoption of the Master's behavioral teachings. Following Christ, in the truest sense of the word, requires acceptance of him as our Savior, repentance of our sins, submission to the laws and ordinances of his gospel, and faithful endurance to the end. Then the promise of great light and life can be fully realized. The context for Jesus' statement, cited above, testifies of this. He made this statement after a woman taken in adultery was brought before him to be judged. This woman, caught in her sin, was promised a life—a new life, a life of no longer walking in darkness—*if* she (and this applies to all who listened to his words) would forsake her sins and in faithful obedience submit to him and his gospel. Only through his atonement and its attendant ordinances and commandments do we experience in mortality the real promise of *light* and *life*. In the Bread of Life discourse, Jesus taught, "I am the living bread which came down from heaven; if any man eat of this bread, he shall live for ever; and the bread that I will give is my flesh, which I will give for the life of the world. . . .

"Except ye eat the flesh of the Son of man, and drink his blood, ye have no life in you.

"Whoso eateth my flesh, and drinketh my blood, hath eternal life; and I will raise him up in the resurrection of the just at the last day" (JST John 6:51, 53–54).

Clearly, Jesus is referring to the life- and light-giving power of his atoning sacrifice and the emblems of it that we know as the sacrament. We follow Jesus and obtain light and life when we submit to the ordinances of baptism and confirmation and renew those ordinances by worthily partaking of the Lord's Supper. There are two specific promises resulting from the Atonement that are contained in those ordinances: (1) the forgiveness of sins and (2) the companionship of the Holy Ghost. In these are found light and life as we sojourn in mortality.

Forgiveness of Sins

Just as the woman taken in adultery was able to receive a new life, so to speak, through her faith in Christ, her repentance, and her continued obedience, we also can be filled with the "light of life" that accompanies a forgiveness of sins. The apostle Paul testified that because of Christ's atoning sacrifice we are able to "walk in newness of life.

"For if we have been planted together in the likeness of his death, we shall be also in the likeness of his resurrection:

"Knowing this, that our old man is crucified with him, that the body of sin might be destroyed, that henceforth we should not serve sin.

"For he that is dead to sin is freed from sin.

"Now if we be dead with Christ, we believe that we shall also live with him:

"Knowing that Christ being raised from the dead dieth no more; death hath no more dominion over him.

"For in that he died, he died unto sin once: but in that he liveth, he liveth unto God.

"Likewise reckon ye also yourselves to be dead indeed unto sin, but *alive unto God through Jesus Christ our Lord*" (JST Romans 6:4–11; emphasis added).

"I am crucified with Christ: nevertheless I live; yet not I, but Christ liveth in me: and the life which I now live in the flesh I live by the faith of the Son of God, who loved me, and gave himself for me" (Galatians 2:20).

Truly, forgiveness of our sins does not merely give us a new lease on life, it gives us a new life—a life in Christ, a life in his light, a life empowered with his power, a life enriched by his love. Without this spiritual life in Christ we are, as C. S. Lewis described it, merely lifeless statues—made with the elements of the earth but lacking real life. When we are born again and become new creatures in Christ, partly through partaking of his atonement, we experience "as big a change as a statue which changed from being a carved stone to being a real man.

"And that is precisely what Christianity is about. This world is a great sculptor's shop. We are the statues and there is a rumour going round the shop that some of us are some day going to come to life."[2]

"Christ, here and now, in that very room where you are saying your prayers, is doing things to you. It is not a question of a good man who died two thousand years ago. It is a living Man, still as much a man as you, and still as much God as He was when He created the world, really coming and interfering with your very self; killing the old natural self in you and replacing it with the kind of self He has. At first, only for moments. Then for longer periods. Finally, if all goes well, turning you permanently into a different sort of thing; into . . . a being which, in its own small way, has the same kind of life as God; which shares His power, joy, knowledge and eternity."[3]

The scriptures speak of this new life as "a mighty change in us, or in our hearts, that we have no more disposition to do evil, but to do good continually" (Mosiah 5:2). President Joseph F. Smith likewise described this newness of life as a change in his desires, direction, and perspective on life. "The feeling that came upon me was that of pure peace, of love and light," he declared. "I felt as if I wanted to do good everywhere to everybody and to everything. I felt a newness of life, a newness of desire to do that which was right. There was not one particle of desire for evil left in my soul."[4] What a life! What fulfillment and purpose and peace!

With a forgiveness of sins that comes when we covenant with Christ through faith, repentance, and baptism—and when we continually repent of our sins and worthily partake of the sacrament—the Lord has "called [us] out of darkness into his marvellous light" (1 Peter 2:9). Even though we live in a world that is filled with darkness and evil, we can be filled with light—his light. What is this "marvellous light," and what can it do for us as we face the challenges of the world each day of our lives? It is the companionship of the Holy Ghost that is promised to every member of the Church each week as we partake of the sacrament of the Lord's Supper—"that they may always have his Spirit to be with them" (Moroni 4:3).

The Companionship of the Holy Ghost

I can think of no greater light to guide us in a darkened and darkening world than the Light of the World himself. While he may not continually go before us as a "pillar of fire" as he did with the ancients, he has promised us something just as brilliant and illuminating—the companionship of the Holy Ghost. In this manner, we too can have a member of the Godhead go before us, as it were, enlightening, guiding, protecting, and comforting us. "And I will pray the Father, and he shall give you another Comforter, that he may abide with you for ever," Jesus told his disciples at the Last Supper. "But the Comforter, which is the Holy Ghost, whom the Father will send in my name, he shall teach you all things, and bring all things to your remembrance, whatsoever I have said unto you" (John 14:16, 26). The gift of the Holy Ghost not only teaches us what we should do (see 2 Nephi 32:5) and warns us of dangers, both physical and spiritual, but it also enlivens us and chases darkness from us (see D&C 93:37). If we abide by its light, "there shall be no darkness in [us]" and our lives will be filled with light and understanding (D&C 88:67). It teaches us how to more profoundly commune with Deity (see 2 Nephi 32:8) and gives us greater understanding of the things of God (see 1 Corinthians 12:8; Mosiah 5:3). The Holy Ghost can fill our lives with love and hope (see Moroni 8:26), peace and joy (see Galatians 5:22), and comfort in times of trial and tribulation (see Acts 9:31). The light and life that comes to us through companionship of the Holy Ghost encompasses each of these, and myriad more blessings. President

John Taylor testified of the fruits that flow into our lives when we receive the spiritual light of life offered us through the Atonement and through obedience to the principles and ordinances of the gospel of Jesus Christ:

"We realize that we have not lost his Holy Spirit; and if we continue to encourage it, it will be in us a spirit of life, light, intelligence, and truth,—in fact, a spirit springing up unto everlasting life. It is the principle embodied in the words of Jesus to the woman of Samaria [see John 4:10–14].

"We feel that we are in possession of the principles of eternal life, which are as a well of water within us and around us, and of which we drink and participate in when we live our religion. It emanates from God, issues from the Fountain of life and truth— the Source of all intelligence, and is imparted to us through the medium of the everlasting Gospel. It has enlightened our minds, enlarged our understandings, extended our feelings, informed our judgment—has warmed up our affections to God and holiness, has nourished and cherished us, and put us in possession of principles that we know will abide for ever and for ever."[5]

As we eat of the Bread of Life and drink the blood of the Lamb of God through worthily partaking of the sacrament and by always remembering him with our whole souls, we will "not walk in darkness, but shall have the light of life"—both in the eternal realms and throughout the darkness of our mortal world. What a great promise! What an abundant life we may come to know! What a bright and shining Light to lead us through the darkness of mortality into the brilliance of eternity! What a profound truth!

"LET YOUR LIGHT SO SHINE"

"Ye are the light of the world," Jesus declared unto the disciples in the Sermon on the Mount (Matthew 5:14). How is it that we as disciples of Christ can be called the "light of the world," seeing that the Savior refers to himself as the "Light and Life of the

World"? What did he mean by that? What is meant by his later injunction: "Let your light so shine before men, that they may see your good works, and glorify your Father which is in heaven" (Matthew 5:16)?

More often than not we look at those scriptural phrases and think that the Savior is telling us to be a good example. Undoubtedly, he is saying that to us, but I believe there is something deeper in that charge. We may sometimes view the phrase, "Let your light so shine" in an all-too-shallow and superficial way—perhaps like our children do when we tell them to let their own lights shine. To them, it means something akin to "Remember who you are" or "Be on your best behavior" or "Remember your manners" or "Don't burp in public!" When we get a glimpse of what Christ as the Life and Light of the World can do *for* us and *to* us, we see that his admonition to let *our light* so shine is something far more encompassing.

The resurrected Christ declared unto the Nephites, "Behold *I am the light which ye shall hold up—that which ye have seen me do*" (3 Nephi 18:24; emphasis added). It is this Light that our lives must reflect in order to lead others to "glorify [their] Father which is in heaven." Letting the Light of Life be reflected in us is the natural by-product of taking Christ's name upon us and having his image graven upon our countenances. Inasmuch as we live our lives in such a way as to, as the Prophet Joseph Smith taught, "let the light of heaven shine through [us] to the view of other men,"[6] we become *a* light of the world, reflecting *the* Light of the World. The degree to which our lives illuminate the way for others will be proportionate to the degree to which the Light of Life radiates in us. His *life* is what gives me my *light*. His *light* is what must be seen in my *life*. A covenanted and consecrated disciple of Christ, will know that it is not his own life—no matter how good his heart or how noble his actions—that is to be put on a candlestick for all to see. It is Jesus who is the Light we must shine forth from our very being. That light—our lives and examples—is but a reflection of what we have allowed Christ, through our faith in him and our willingness to follow him, to do to us and for us. "He that hath the Son *hath life*," John the Beloved testified (1 John 5:12; emphasis added). Therefore, "let us walk in the light of the Lord" (Isaiah 2:5).

Notes

1. See Craig S. Keener, *A Commentary on the Gospel of Matthew* (Grand Rapids, Mich.: Eerdmans Publishing Co., 1999), 302–4.

2. C. S. Lewis, *Mere Christianity* (New York: Macmillan, 1952), 140.

3. Ibid., 164.

4. Joseph F. Smith, *Gospel Doctrine* (Salt Lake City: Deseret Book, 1939), 96.

5. John Taylor, *Journal of Discourses*, 26 vols. (London: Latter-day Saints' Book Depot, 1854–86), 7:318.

6. Joseph Smith, as quoted in Thomas S. Monson, in Conference Report, August 1971 (British Area General Conference), 145.

CHAPTER 10

"WATCH AND BE READY"

One of my favorite Primary songs when I was growing up was "When He Comes Again," by Mirla Greenwood Thayne. I think its lyrics capture the feelings of wonder that we all share concerning the Second Coming.

> *I wonder, when he comes again,*
> *Will herald angels sing?*
> *Will earth be white with drifted snow,*
> *Or will the world know spring?*
> *I wonder if one star will shine*
> *Far brighter than the rest;*
> *Will daylight stay the whole night through?*
> *Will songbirds leave their nests?*
> *I'm sure he'll call his little ones*
> *Together round his knee,*
> *Because he said in days gone by,*
> *"Suffer them to come to me."*[1]

Unfortunately, I have seen how the innocent "wondering" described in that song can, if not guarded against, swell to fruitless speculation that dangerously distracts individuals from their spiritual missions or creates unhealthy anxiety that destroys faith and hope and leaves them fearful of the future.

When I began my teaching career many years ago it was customary to begin seminary classes with a brief devotional conducted by students. Most of the time these devotionals were nice but not necessary, and rarely were they remarkable. Once in a while, however, a student would deliver a memorable spiritual thought or do something that would really stick with the students. One of the latter—the type that really sticks—was delivered by a young man who typically didn't say much in class and rarely, if ever, had participated in class devotionals. His father had shared with this boy something he had received in his high priest's group the previous Sunday. It was so interesting to the boy that he wanted everyone in the seminary class to have a copy of it.

We had been studying the New Testament in seminary that year and so he made the necessary connection between his spiritual thought and what we had studied. "Jesus said that nobody, not even the angels, knows when the Second Coming will be," this young man stated. "Well, that may have been true in Jesus' day, but *now we know!*" Boy, that got my attention! He then distributed the handout to each member of the class and went through it point by point. I don't remember everything that was on it, but it was someone's "calculations" of when the Savior's second coming would occur. Some of it was based on scriptural prophecies, but much of it came from tradition (or what could be characterized as Mormon folklore) or speculations that I had never heard before. Many of the signs and calculations that led up to the end prediction were so unbelievable they were laughable; and I almost did laugh as this student read through the handout with the class. But I didn't because I didn't want to embarrass him and I could see that the students were very interested and very serious about what he was saying.

The bottom line to all of these speculations was that the Second Coming would occur on April 6, 1996—which seemed a long time away at that moment. The students were excited by what they had heard and could talk of nothing else the rest of the class. It was not long until this handout was being circulated in various classes and quorums in many wards and stakes. It spread like wildfire throughout the entire area.

April 6, 1996, has come and gone, and we have not witnessed the Second Coming (as far as I know). Yet, over the years, I have continued to come across similar "calculations" and attempts to nail down the exact date of the second coming of Christ. "We may not know the day or the hour," some have stated, "but we can know the year." With almost every major world event, such as devastating earthquakes, floods, or famines throughout the world, I hear people say, "This is it! The Second Coming is right around the corner!" Political events on the world stage generate speculation and what I call "Second Coming anxiety." At the outbreak of the Gulf War in 1991, for example, I heard members of the Church speculate that the war was the battle of Armageddon and would culminate in the destruction of the wicked and the glorious return of the Savior. With the close of 1999 and the dawn of a new millennium came all kinds of sensational speculations, both in and out of the Church, regarding the Second Coming, the end of the world, and what many Christians call the "Rapture." It seems that there is always someone who thinks he has a new scientific method—such as the exponential increase in earthquakes, hurricanes, tornadoes, or other natural disasters—or some secret key to prophetic interpretation that allows him to predict the Second Coming.

"Can we use this scientific data to extrapolate that the Second Coming is likely to occur during the next few years, or the next decade, or the next century?" Elder M. Russell Ballard of the Quorum of the Twelve Apostles asked. He then proceeded to answer his own question: "Not really. I am called as one of the apostles to be a special witness of Christ in these exciting, trying times, and I do not know when He is going to come again. As far as I know, none of my brethren in the Council of the Twelve or even in the First Presidency know. And I would humbly suggest to you . . . that if we do not know, then nobody knows, no matter how compelling their arguments or how reasonable their calculations. The Savior said that 'of that day and hour knoweth no man, no, not the angels of heaven, but my Father only' (Matthew 24:36).

"I believe that when the Lord says 'no man' knows, it really means that no man knows. You should be extremely wary of anyone who claims to be an exception to divine decree."[2]

Perhaps more than any other doctrinal subject discussed in my religion classes at BYU, the subject of the signs of the times and the Second Coming elicits many questions and much discussion. It seems that we want the Lord to give us a chronological chart of the signs that will precede the Second Coming, thus resulting in our ability to predict with precision the date of the Lord's return. "Why are you so interested in knowing when the Second Coming will be?" I often ask my classes. "Would it make that much of a difference in your life if you knew the exact date?" After much discussion, it usually boils down to the fact that, as natural men and women, we enjoy speculating and our interest is piqued with sensationalism.

It is kind of like sheepishly looking at all of the sensational (and often outrageous) headlines on the tabloid newspapers lining the checkout stand in the grocery store—"Inquiring minds want to know." Now, don't get me wrong! I am not equating the prophecies concerning the second coming of Christ with the tabloids—far from it. But I do find it interesting that even though Jesus has declared that "of that day and hour knoweth no man, no, not the angels of heaven," we act like we can figure it out if we examine the prophecies more deeply or with some new light. Are we not to watch for the signs? Yes, of course! We are to search the prophecies found in the scriptures. We should take heed of the signs of the times, paying particular attention to their fulfillment. But to do that in an effort to predict the date of the Second Coming is looking beyond the mark and entirely misses the point Jesus was teaching his ancient disciples on the Mount of Olives in Matthew, chapter 24. The message of this great discourse has also been reiterated for modern Saints in this dispensation in both the Joseph Smith Translation and the Doctrine and Covenants.

As I ask my students why they are so curious about the signs of the last days, invariably someone will say, "Because we want to know how much time we have left to sin before we need to repent." The comment is intended to be humorous and is usually met with laughter and good-natured kidding. Unfortunately, there tends to be a lot of truth in that comment. That kind of attitude, likewise, misses the point of Jesus' prophetic teachings. He didn't say "watch" for the signs for curiosity's sake or so that you can have some inside information. Neither did he say, "Take heed to the signs, so you will know when to repent." He said: "Watch therefore: for ye know not what hour your Lord doth come" (Matthew 24:42). In addition to his admonition to watch the signs, he added this important charge: "Therefore be ye also ready" (Matthew 24:44). The Savior's teachings concerning the Last Days and the Second Coming seem to deal with two things: (1) *when* he will come again and (2) *what* we must do to be ready for that grand and glorious day.

WHEN WILL THE SAVIOR COME AGAIN?

"Tell us, when shall these things be?" the disciples asked the Savior, "and what shall be the sign of thy coming, and of the end of the world?" (Matthew 24:3). They, like we do today, wanted the Master to give an exact date (or at least narrow it down to within a few weeks). He answered their question, but not in the way they expected or wanted. In this dispensation, he has done the same thing again and again, but we, like the ancient disciples, aren't satisfied with the answer and desire something more specific.

As I have thought about this episode in the New Testament

and observed the almost all-consuming interest some modern Saints have concerning the signs of Jesus' second coming, a parallel comes to mind—a parallel to which every parent who has ever traveled with small children can relate. "How much farther, Daddy?" "Are we there yet?" "When will we be there?" "Is that it?" I have heard those questions and myriad more like them more times than I care to remember. I learned as a father (and experienced as a child, but didn't fully understand) that no answer, no matter how specific or precise, can adequately satisfy the child. I don't think, for example, that a three-year-old can comprehend and thus cease asking, "How much farther?" if I were to say: "We have one thousand one hundred and eighty-seven miles until we arrive at Disneyland." Even answers like, "We'll be there in about an hour" (or even fifteen minutes) can't satisfy a child whose excitement is unbounded and whose attention span is slightly less than a nanosecond. In a way, we are like children. Answers have been given, but they don't satisfy us because we cannot comprehend the Lord's second coming timetable any better than little children can understand hours and minutes, miles and landmarks, or signals and road signs along the road.

In his discourse to the disciples on the Mount of Olives, the Savior answered their questions with signs to look for, but reminded them that no one—not even the angels in heaven—know the exact date of his coming. It appears to me that the Lord is telling us we will not know exactly the *when* until it occurs. This just wasn't what the disciples wanted and expected to hear and they couldn't fully fathom what they did hear. But it was the right answer anciently. It is still the right answer today.

In this dispensation, the Lord has reiterated what he taught anciently and has provided many additional insights. In the Doctrine and Covenants, he has reminded us that we are living in the "eleventh hour" before the Second Coming (see D&C 33:3). We are told that his coming "is near, even at the doors" (D&C

110:16). And that was in 1836! Just think how near it must be now! Thirteen times in the Doctrine and Covenants the Savior states, "I come quickly." He describes his second coming as "nigh at hand" another twelve times and as "soon" six times. (So I think we can safely surmise that it is "nigher at hand" and "sooner" than it was before.) Despite all of this, he clearly teaches us that no one knows exactly *when* that great event will occur (see D&C 39:21; 49:7; 51:20; 61:38; 124:10; 133:11).

Nothing illustrates this better than an experience from the life of the Prophet Joseph. He recounted this experience in 1843, although it had occurred years earlier.

"I was once praying very earnestly to know the time of the coming of the Son of Man, when I heard a voice repeat the following:

"Joseph, my son, if thou livest until thou art eighty-five years old, thou shalt see the face of the Son of Man; therefore *let this suffice, and trouble me no more on this matter.*

"I was left thus, without being able to decide whether this coming referred to the beginning of the millennium or to some previous appearing, or whether I should die and thus see his face.

"I believe the coming of the Son of Man will not be any sooner than that time" (D&C 130:14–17, emphasis added).

What did the Lord mean by that? Didn't he know when Joseph would die? Of course he did! I believe that he was telling the Prophet that knowing the *when* isn't very important. I can almost hear the Savior saying, "I have already given you the answer to your question. Let this suffice. Don't worry so much about it! You have more important things that should occupy your attention and devotion. So, don't bother me anymore about an exact date. I've told you all I will right now. Now, go about doing what you are supposed to be doing." I think that is what he was also trying to teach his ancient disciples who desired to know *when* he would return. Of course, they probably wanted an exact day, month, and year, not a principle to live by.

In Luke's account of Jesus' Olivet discourse, an interesting parable is included (see Luke 12:34–48). It was intended to teach the disciples to be watchful, prayerful, and ever prepared for the Second Coming. In the parable, the disciples are likened to servants who are to watch over the household (the Church) while the master (Christ) attends a wedding feast (ascends to heaven). They have their assigned tasks, and if they are found faithful when the master returns they will be invited to join the master at a final feast (inherit celestial glory). The Joseph Smith Translation of these verses provides us with an important insight—that the Savior's coming, as it were, comes at different times to different people.

"For, behold, *he cometh in the first watch of the night, and he shall also come in the second watch, and again he shall come in the third watch.*

"*And verily I say unto you, He hath already come*, as it is written of him; and again when he shall come in the second watch, or come in the third watch, blessed are those servants when he cometh, that he shall find so doing;

"For the Lord of those servants shall gird himself, and make them to sit down to meat, and will come forth and serve them.

"And now, verily I say these things unto you, that ye may know this, that the coming of the Lord is as a thief in the night. . . .

"And he said unto them, Verily I say unto you, be ye therefore ready also; for the Son of Man cometh at an hour when ye think not" (JST Luke 12:41–44, 47; emphasis added).

Commenting on these passages from the Joseph Smith Translation, Elder Bruce R. McConkie stated that "these sayings of Jesus give a new and added concept to the teaching that men should watch, pray, and be ready for the Second Coming; they outline a concept which is not elsewhere set forth with the clarity and plainness here recorded. . . .

"All of the Lord's ministers, all of the members of his Church, and for that matter all men everywhere ('What I say unto one, I say unto all'), are counseled to await with righteous readiness the coming of the Lord. However, most men will die before he comes, and only those then living will rejoice or tremble, as the case may be, at his personal presence. But all who did prepare will be rewarded *as though they had lived when he came*, while the wicked will be 'cut asunder' and appointed their 'portion with the hypocrites' as surely *as though they lived in the very day of dread and vengeance*.

"Thus, in effect, the Lord comes in every watch of the night, on every occasion when men are called to face death and judgment."[3]

The Lord, in the Doctrine and Covenants, uses a phrase similar to that used when he referred to the Second Coming occurring "in such an hour as ye think not" (Matthew 24:44). "Hearken unto my voice," the Lord declares, "lest death shall overtake you; *in an hour when ye think not* the summer shall be past, and the harvest ended, and your souls not saved" (D&C 45:2; emphasis added). It is clear that what the Lord wants us to understand concerning the *when* of the Second Coming is that knowing the date or seeing the signs means little when compared to being spiritually prepared. Likewise, life or death does not determine the greatness or dreadfulness of that day. It is our righteousness or wickedness that counts.

After I have shared these scriptures and taught this concept to my own students at BYU, I then follow up with this question: "Now, do you want to know the exact day when the Savior will come?" The students usually shake their heads no and say, "We don't know the exact day"—demonstrating that they have heard and understood what I have taught. Then I push them a little more. "I am serious," I say. "I can tell you the exact day when the Savior will come. And I will show you in the scriptures. You can go home and tell your roommates and write it in your journal. I can tell you the exact day." That gets their attention (even though some laugh and think I am joking)! Then we turn to the sixty-fourth section of the Doctrine and Covenants and read the Lord's own words.

"Behold, now *it is called today until the coming of the Son of Man*, and verily it is a day of sacrifice, and a day for the tithing of my people; for he that is tithed shall not be burned at his coming.

"For *after today cometh the burning*—this is speaking after the manner of the Lord—for verily I say, *tomorrow all the proud and they that do wickedly shall be as stubble*; and I will burn them up, for I am the Lord of Hosts; and I will not spare any that remain in Babylon" (D&C 64:23–24; emphasis added).

"When will the Lord come?" I ask again. "What is the exact day (notice I didn't say date)?" They all respond, "Tomorrow." That is the right answer—straight from the mouth of the Lord himself. We can rest assured that the Lord will come *tomorrow*; and we need to be preparing and worthy *today*—each day, every day, no matter how long today is. What an important concept! The Lord reminds us: "Wherefore, if ye believe me, *ye will labor while it is called today*" (D&C 64:25; emphasis added). Well, since we now know *when*—*tomorrow*—let us devote ourselves to the greater issue of *what*—what we must do to prepare *today*. As President Gordon B. Hinckley declared:

"Certainly there is no point in speculating concerning the day and the hour. Let us rather live each day so that if the Lord does come while we are yet upon the earth we shall be worthy of that change which will occur as in the twinkling of an eye and under which we shall be changed from mortal to immortal beings. And if we should die before he comes, then—if our lives have conformed to his teachings—we shall arise in that resurrection morning and be partakers of the marvelous experiences designed for those who shall live and work with the Savior in that promised Millennium. We need not fear the day of his coming; the very purpose of the Church is to provide the incentive and the opportunity for us to conduct our lives in such a way that those who are members of the kingdom of God will become members of the kingdom of heaven when he establishes that kingdom on earth."[4]

WHAT MUST WE DO TO BE PREPARED FOR THE SECOND COMING?

One of the rules of effective communication is to answer the question that should have been asked, not just the one that was asked. Jesus effectively utilized this principle on many occasions—answering questions but also teaching broader principles and concepts that his listeners needed to hear, even if they didn't ask for them. One such example is Jesus' response to the disciples' query concerning his second coming. "When shall these things be?" they asked. He answered that specific question by giving the signs of his coming and repeatedly reminding them that no one knows the exact time of that event. He didn't stop there, however. There was more that these disciples needed to hear, even though they didn't ask. It is almost as if Jesus were saying, "I've answered your question, but there is another question you didn't ask that is far more important: *What must we do to be prepared for that day?* The answer to that question is more important (even essential) than the answers I've already given you." The rest of Jesus' discourse on the Mount of Olives dealt with that question.

Similarly, in modern revelation, he has given us more specific information about the necessary preparations than he has about the prophetic signs of his coming. Both go hand in hand, but one (knowing the signs) is *interesting*, maybe even important, and the other (personal preparation) is *imperative*. "Be ye also ready," was and is the Savior's charge to his disciples. How can we be ready and not be overtaken by spiritual slumber that will leave us unprepared and unworthy at his coming?

Treasure up the words of the Lord and his servants. In the Joseph Smith Translation of Matthew, chapter 24, the Savior warned of "false Christs, and false prophets [who] shall show great signs and wonders, insomuch, that, if possible, they shall deceive the very elect, who are the elect according to the covenant" (Joseph Smith–Matthew 1:22). That is a frightening thought that can further exacerbate "Second Coming anxiety." Yet it need not paralyze us with fear, because the Lord, with the warning, provides hope with his counsel and a promise of protection. "And whoso treasureth up my word, shall not be deceived" (Joseph Smith–Matthew 1:37). Treasuring up the words of the Lord means much more than simply reading the scriptures. Treasuring means embracing them—studying and pondering their words and living by their precepts. It means making the words of the Lord *our* words, the words *we* live by, the compass that guides *our* footsteps in *our* journey through life. Treasuring up the words of the Lord requires us to internalize the doctrines of Christ, not just read them, think about them, or discuss them in our classes and quorums. They must become a living, vibrant part of us. As we treasure up the scriptures in our hearts, minds, and souls we discover that there is a protective power in them far more significant than intellectual understanding or being able to perceive fulfillment of the prophetic word. There is a real power, a protective power and a guiding light, in the words of God. Although President Ezra Taft Benson was speaking specifically of the Book of Mormon, his words and promises can be generalized to include all of the standard works:

"It is not just that the Book of Mormon teaches us truth, though indeed it does that. It is not just that the Book of Mormon bears testimony of Christ, though it indeed does that, too. But there is something more. There is a power in the book which will begin to flow into your lives the moment you begin a serious study of the book. You will find greater power to resist temptation. You will find the power to avoid deception. You will find the power to stay on the strait and narrow path."[5]

We are blessed not only to have the standard works to help prepare us for the Second Coming, but also "living scriptures"— protective instructions, exhortations, testimonies, and promises— that we should also treasure as we prepare to meet the Lord. These come to us from the Lord's anointed servants—those possessing the keys of the kingdom and sustained and set apart as prophets, seers, and revelators—in these last days. As they speak "when moved upon by the Holy Ghost," their words "shall be scripture, shall be the will of the Lord, shall be the mind of the Lord, shall be the word of the Lord, shall be the voice of the Lord, and the power of God unto salvation" (D&C 68:4).

It is interesting to note that in this same revelation the Lord speaks of these servants as those to whom "it shall be given to know the signs of the times, and the signs of the coming of the Son of Man" (D&C 68:11). We can look not only to the scriptures but also to the living prophets to help us to recognize the signs of the times and to prepare for the Second Coming. Just as the ancient disciples sat at the feet of the Savior on the Mount of Olives and received answers to their questions and important counsel regarding spiritual readiness, we too can sit at the feet of the Savior, as it were, as we hearken to the words of the Lord's anointed. They, like the Savior, may not give us all the answers we think we have to have regarding the *when* questions. We may not always like it when they say, "I don't know," but we must keep our eyes fixed on them and our ears attuned to their words. They may not have the answers to all our questions, but they are continually answering the question we should be most interested in: How can we be prepared for the great and dreadful day of the Lord? Their words teach us *what* we must do and be to be prepared to joyfully greet the bridegroom when he comes again. The degree to which we "treasure" their words and hearken to their counsel is the degree to which we will be protected and prepared in the last days. "Your safety and ours," President Harold B. Lee taught, "depends upon whether or not we follow the ones whom the Lord has placed to preside over his church."[6]

Oil lamps filled with "reservoirs of righteousness." In teaching the disciples about the need to watch and be ready for the Second Coming, the Savior used three unique parables. We are perhaps most familiar with the parable of the ten virgins. The foolish virgins were unprepared to greet the bridegroom. His coming was delayed and they ran out of oil. The wise virgins were prepared because they brought additional oil for their lamps. Much has been said and written about this parable through the generations. It is not my intent to provide new interpretations or additional commentary. Rather, it is important to highlight a few of the relevant themes that have practical application to us today. Clearly, the Lord is reiterating that his coming will not occur when it is most expected or most convenient. Therefore, we are to be in a state of constant readiness—spiritual preparation cannot be done hastily at the last minute. There is no crash course, no Cliffs Notes® for spiritual preparation. It requires consistent, continual, conscientious effort. Similarly, the parable seems to be telling us that the kind of oil we need in our lamps to be prepared to meet the Master cannot be hastily purchased at the store at the last minute or borrowed from someone else. It is something that one must acquire individually. "The foolish asked the others to share their oil, but spiritual preparedness cannot be shared in an instant," wrote President Spencer W. Kimball. "The wise had to go, else the bridegroom would have gone unwelcomed. They needed all their oil for themselves; they could not save the foolish. The responsibility was each for himself.

"This was not selfishness or unkindness. The kind of oil that is needed to illuminate the way and light up darkness is not shareable.

How can one share obedience to the principle of tithing; a mind at peace from righteous living; an accumulation of knowledge? How can one share faith or testimony? How can one share attitudes or chastity, or the experience of a mission? How can one share temple privileges? Each must obtain that kind of oil for himself.

"The foolish virgins were not averse to buying oil. They knew they should have oil. They merely procrastinated, not knowing when the bridegroom would come.

"In the parable, oil can be purchased at the market. In our lives the oil of preparedness is accumulated drop by drop in righteous living. Attendance at sacrament meetings adds oil to our lamps drop by drop over the years. Fasting, family prayer, home teaching, control of bodily appetites, preaching the gospel, studying the scriptures—each act of dedication and obedience is a drop added to our store. Deeds of kindness, payment of offerings and tithes, chaste thoughts and actions, marriage in the covenant for eternity—these, too, contribute importantly to the oil with which we can at midnight refuel our exhausted lamps."[7]

We don't have to know *when* the Savior will come to be prepared. We don't even have to know all the signs and prophecies concerning the last days to begin keeping the commandments. Simply stated, living the gospel day by day, repenting when we sin, doing a little better today than yesterday, becoming a little better person each day, living the "golden rule" and loving the Lord is what fills our oil lamps. We may not even know how full our lamps are at any given time, but as we live the gospel each day we are adding to, what President Kimball called, our "reservoirs of righteousness."[8]

With this kind of continual devotion, our oil lamps will always be trimmed and burning bright. The lamps of the wise virgins are not just decorations to celebrate the coming of the Lord. With lamps burning bright, "wise virgins" will have light to illuminate their path and guide their lives no matter how long they must wait for the bridegroom. "For they that are wise and have received the truth," the Lord declared, "and *have taken the Holy Spirit for their guide*, and have not been deceived—verily I say unto you, they shall not be hewn down and cast into the fire, but shall abide the day" (D&C 45:57; emphasis added). Daily living of our lives in such a way as to be worthy of the companionship of the Holy Ghost is the best way to be prepared for the Second Coming. Living worthy of and hearkening to the Spirit keeps our lamps continually full of the oil of spiritual preparation.

Anxiously engaged in service to God and fellowmen. After Jesus taught the disciples the parable of the ten virgins and admonished them to "watch therefore, for ye know neither the day nor the hour wherein the Son of man cometh" (Matthew 25:13), he shared two other parables about preparing for the Second Coming. These are known as the parable of the talents (Matthew 25:14–30) and the parable of the sheep and the goats (Matthew 25:31–46). They are lesser known than the parable of the ten virgins and are not usually taught in the context of preparing for the Savior's return. But they were given in that specific context—teaching the disciples how to "watch and be ready."

The first parable deals with "a man traveling into a far country" (Christ returning to heaven). He gives his servants (us) differing amounts of talents (spiritual abilities and responsibilities) and charges them to be good stewards while he is gone. He promises to return and take an accounting of what they have done with their talents. "After a long time the lord of those servants cometh, and reckoneth with them" (Matthew 25:19). Those who "multiplied" their talents were rewarded when the Master returned and he that "buried" his talent was condemned. I have heard this parable taught in many different settings, with many different interpretations. I am sure that it can apply to utilizing our God-given talents, such as music or art, so we don't lose those abilities. It probably also has application to the need we all have to magnify our callings in the Church. (It may even have a financial application to investments and dividends.) However, I don't think that is exactly what the Lord had in mind.

It appears to me that what the Lord is saying about preparing for the Second Coming is that we should be anxiously engaged in utilizing, in his service, the gifts, abilities, and testimonies the Lord has bestowed upon us. While he is "away" we all have responsibilities to attend to in his vineyard. We may have differing gifts and the sizes of our tasks may vary, but the Lord expects us not to "bury" our talents—either by idling away our talents in "all is well in Zion" complacence or failing to be faithful because of hand-wringing anxiety about the future. The servant who was condemned did nothing because he feared. Those who were rewarded were found faithfully doing what they could—whether much or little—to further the kingdom. "Well done, thou good and faithful servant," the Lord said to those who had done what was expected of them: "Thou hast been faithful over a few things, I will make thee ruler over many things: enter thou into the joy of thy lord" (Matthew 25:21). Whether we are presidents or Primary teachers, apostles or nursery workers, we prepare for the Lord by doing our respective duties, serving the Lord to the best of our abilities, blessing our families, and loving our neighbors.

That leads to the last parable—the sheep and the goats. At the Savior's second coming there will be a great division of the people, like a shepherd separating the sheep from the goats at the end of the day. At his coming, the Good Shepherd will gather his faithful sheep to his right side. To them that day will be a great and glorious day. To his left side will be gathered the goats—those who are not worthy of his presence, those who have not prepared for that day. To them his coming will be a dreadful day. Of those on his right hand the King declares, "Come, ye blessed of my Father, inherit the kingdom prepared for you from the foundation of the world" (Matthew 25:34).

Those who inherit such a reward at the Master's return are those who have fed him when he was hungry, clothed him when he was naked, strengthened him when he was sick, and befriended him when he was a stranger or lonely. How did they do this? "Inasmuch as ye have done it unto one of the least of these my brethren," the Savior declared, "ye have done it unto me" (Matthew 25:40). We prepare to joyfully meet the Savior upon his glorious return with every act of service, compassion, kindness, and mercy. The degree to which we love and serve our fellowmen is the degree to which we are prepared for the Second Coming. We may not notice all the signs around us. We may not understand all of the prophecies concerning the last days. We can, however, notice the suffering and need all around us and do something to ease pain, lighten burdens, lift spirits, and offer hope. It may not require extraordinary efforts or monumental service, but little by little, deed by deed, kindness by kindness, we make the world a better place. And, after all, that is really how we become prepared to meet the Lord and inherit a "better world."

I return to an analogy I used earlier in discussing the questions and anxiety created by fixating on the *when* of the Second Coming. The best way to quiet the questions of "How much farther?" or "Are we there yet?" is to occupy children's attention on more profitable activities and endeavors. The trip seems shorter when our minds and efforts are focused on something other than waiting and wondering how much longer we have. This seems to be what the Lord would have us do, as well. If we will go about doing our duty, filling our oil lamps day by day, loving God and serving our fellowmen, we will be prepared. We will not only witness the remarkable fulfillment of prophecy concerning the Last Days, but we will be actively involved in the unfolding destiny of the Church as the gospel spreads to every people and temples fill the earth. Apprehension and anxiety will disappear. Peace and optimism will govern our lives. Faith will cause fear to flee. "If ye are prepared ye shall not fear," the Lord has promised (D&C 38:30). Our attention, our duty and devotion should be, as President Brigham Young declared, "centered upon this one thing, the sanctification of our own hearts, the purifying of our own affections, the preparing of ourselves for the approach of the events that are hastening upon us. This should be our concern, this should be our study, this should be our daily prayer."⁹ If we will do this, the Second Coming and our involvement in that glorious day will take care of itself.

"Great Shall Be the Glory of His Presence"

A few years ago I had a very distraught student in my office disturbed by something that was stated (or not stated) in her patriarchal blessing. "My blessing doesn't say I will be alive at the Second Coming," she said. "We have been told that we are the 'Saturday's Warriors' and it will be in our generation, but I won't be there." I tried the best I could to comfort her. I told her that my blessing doesn't say I will be alive at the Second Coming either. I don't think that consoled her much. I told her what we know and what we don't know about when the Second Coming would occur. She was afraid that her blessing was saying that she would die young— before the Second Coming.

"You can't make that assumption," I said. "You can't draw conclusions by what the patriarch *didn't* say." But my words did not seem to convince her. I told her there are lots of things about the last days and the Second Coming that I *don't* know. (She was convinced of that point!)

Finally, all I could do was to bear my testimony of what I *do* know concerning the Second Coming. "I don't know when it will be," I stated. "I don't know if you or I will be alive or dead when it occurs. What I do know is that if I am worthy I will not only see the Second Coming, but I will be caught up to meet the Savior and come with him. It doesn't matter when he comes. It doesn't matter whether I am dead or alive. All that matters is if I have lived a worthy life. That is what prepares me for that day." I don't know if my words eased her concerns, but I know they are true! There is little profit in wondering too much about *when* he comes again, but there is in examining ourselves—our spiritual preparation, our personal worthiness, our devotion to God, and our love for our fellowmen.

I wonder, when he comes again,
Will I be ready there
To look upon his loving face
And join with him in prayer?
Each day I'll try to do his will
And let my light so shine
That others seeing me may seek
For greater light divine.
Then, when that blessed day is here,
He'll love me and he'll say,
"You've served me well, my little child;
Come unto my arms to stay."[10]

The Savior's message for us is to labor and love, serve and sacrifice, and work and worship *today*, so that when he comes *tomorrow* we will be ready. It is as simple as that. I don't know when that tomorrow will come, but what a tomorrow it will be! I look forward to it with love and longing. "And so great shall be the glory of his presence" (D&C 133:49). Oh how I want to be there! "For since the beginning of the world have not men heard nor perceived by the ear, neither hath any eye seen," the scriptures attest, "how great things [God] hast prepared for him that waiteth for [the Lord]" (D&C 133:45). Oh what promises are in store for those who have "waited for the Lord" whether in life or in death!

"He will swallow up death in victory; and the Lord God will wipe away tears from off all faces; and the rebuke of his people shall he take away from off all the earth: for the Lord hath spoken it.

"And it shall be said in that day, Lo, this is our God; we have waited for him, and he will save us: this is the Lord; we have waited for him, we will be glad and rejoice in his salvation" (Isaiah 25:8–9).

"Therefore are they before the throne of God, and serve him day and night in his temple: and he that sitteth on the throne shall dwell among them.

"They shall hunger no more, neither thirst any more; neither shall the sun light on them, nor any heat.

"For the Lamb which is in the midst of the throne shall feed them, *and shall lead them unto living fountains of waters:* and God shall wipe away all tears from their eyes" (Revelation 7:15–17; emphasis added).

May we drink deeply of the living waters the Savior offers us *today* so that we can partake of the Fountain of Living Waters in that glorious *tomorrow* and forever.

Notes

1. Mirla Greenwood Thayne, "When He Comes Again," *Children's Songbook* (Salt Lake City: The Church of Jesus Christ of Latter-day Saints, 1989), 82–83.
2. M. Russell Ballard, "When Shall These Things Be?" in *Brigham Young University 1995–96 Speeches* (Provo, Utah: Brigham Young University, 1996), 186.
3. Bruce R. McConkie, *Doctrinal New Testament Commentary*, 3 vols. (Salt Lake City: Bookcraft, 1965–73), 1:676–77.
4. Gordon B. Hinckley, *Teachings of Gordon B. Hinckley* (Salt Lake City: Deseret Book, 1997), 576.
5. Ezra Taft Benson, *A Witness and a Warning* (Salt Lake City: Deseret Book, 1988), 21–22.
6. Harold B. Lee, in Conference Report, October 1970, 153.
7. Spencer W. Kimball, *Faith Precedes the Miracle* (Salt Lake City: Deseret Book, 1972), 255–56.
8. Ibid., 109–14.

9. Brigham Young, *Journal of Discourses*, 26 vols. (London: Latter-day Saints' Book Depot, 1854–86), 9:3.

10. Thayne, "When He Comes Again," 82–83.

INDEX